TEARS OFTEN SHED

CHILD HEALTH AND WELFARE
IN AUSTRALIA FROM 1788

BRYAN GANDEVIA, M.D., F.R.A.C.P.
Fellow of the Faculty for the History and
Philosophy of Medicine and Pharmacy,
Worshipful Society of Apothecaries, London

With the research assistance of
SHEILA SIMPSON, B.Sc., Dip.Lib., A.L.A.A.

PERGAMON PRESS

By the same author

An Annotated Bibliography of the History of
  Medicine in Australia
Occupation and Disease in Australia since 1788
The Melbourne Medical Students 1862-1942

First published 1978

Pergamon Press (Australia) Pty Ltd, 19a Boundary Street, Rushcutters Bay NSW 2011
A. Wheaton & Company, A Division of Pergamon Press, Hennock Road, Exeter, EX2 BRP
Pergamon Press Ltd, Headington Hill Hall, Oxford OX3 OBW
Pergamon Press Inc, Maxwell House, Fairview Park, Elmsford, New York 10523
Pergamon of Canada Ltd, 75 The East Mall, Toronto, Ontario M8Z 2L9, Canada
Pergamon Press GmbH, 6242 Kronberg/Taunus, Pferdstrasse 1, Frankfurt-am-Main,
West Germany
Pergamon Press SARL 24 rue des Ecoles, 75240 Paris, Cedex 05, France
Second impression 1978

© Bryan Gandevia 1977

National Library of Australia
Cataloguing in publication data

Gandevia, Bryan
  Tears often shed.

  Index.
  Bibliography.
  ISBN 0 08 023159 4

  1. Child welfare — Australia. 2. Children —
  care and hygiene. I. Simpson, Sheila. II. Title.

362.7'0994

Designed by Charter Books Pty. Ltd., Gordon
Typeset in Australia by G.T. Setters Pty. Ltd., Lane Cove
Printed in Australia by Knudsen Printing Pty. Ltd., Waterloo

TEARS OFTEN SHED

CHILD HEALTH AND WELFARE
IN AUSTRALIA FROM 1788

And really, if you was to see … the tears that are
often shed upon the infants at the breast, you must have feelings
that otherwise you never could have any experience of.

*Letter from a young man at
Port Jackson*, April 1790

Our first child took, in days like these,
A cruel week in dyin',
All day upon her father's knees,
Or on my poor breast lyin';
The tears we shed — the prayers we said
Were awful, wild — despairin'!
I've pulled three through and buried two
Since then — and I'm past carin'.

H. Lawson, *Past Carin'*, 1899

Foreword

by Sir Lorimer Dods, M.V.O., M.D., Ch.M.(Syd.), D.C.H.(Lond.), F.R.A.C.P.
Emeritus Professor of Child Health, University of Sydney

Bryan Gandevia's personal and unceasing interest in the history of Australian medicine had its beginnings more than 30 years ago while he was still a medical student in the University of Melbourne and has been responsible for the publication of many outstanding contributions in this field. His remarkably wide knowledge of this subject is clearly revealed in this most impressive review of child health and welfare in Australia written with particular reference to the early years of the first settlement at Port Jackson and the translation of an essentially European society to a new and strange environment: a review which serves to underline his belief that children, their health and their welfare, represent a particularly sensitive index of the adaptation of a society to its environment.

As he has stated in his preface, this is not a history of Australian paediatrics, but essentially the story of the adaptation of Australia's children to a new world, both physical and social, an adaptation which had its beginnings in the crowded convict ships and in the early struggling penal colony of Sydney Cove.

He has drawn attention to the rather surprising absence in this new and struggling settlement of the usual infectious diseases of infancy and childhood, and has pointed out that these infections apparently could not survive the six or seven months of isolation in a small shipboard world. In this respect, it is interesting to learn that the earliest infectious hazards for Port Jackson's infants were gonorrhoea and syphilis which were followed a little later in the colony's history by gastroenteritis and, later still, by pertussis, which appears to have been the most successful survivor of the long sea voyage.

It is intriguing to find that, despite all the problems of this primitive new settlement, its infant mortality was lower than in the

British Isles, and its steady decline during the early years of the colony suggests the favourable adaptation of its new inhabitants.

In describing the so-called 'female factories', which provided accommodation and care for pregnant, unemployed convict women before and after delivery, the author points out that these institutions represented Australia's first and very primitive obstetric and paediatric hospitals, although their medical functions were far removed from their original purposes as 'houses of correction'.

It seems that for those infants who survived their earliest years in this new colony the greatest hazard was an accident of some sort, and it is noteworthy that the overall pattern of these accidents was not very different from that of today.

By the first decade of the twentieth century an increasing awareness of paediatric problems had led to many varied publications on this subject and to the gradual evolution of specialisation in paediatrics, although few men could rely solely on this type of practice which, like obstetrics, belonged in that era mainly to the family doctor.

Professor Gandevia's outstanding contribution to our knowledge of the earlier stages of child health and welfare in Australia, which will be of inestimable value to students of this subject for many years to come, has been produced to coincide with the first birthday of Sydney's new Prince of Wales Children's Hospital which, under Professor John Beveridge's able leadership, has established itself as a most successful paediatric institution.

Lorimer Dods

Preface

Children, their health and welfare, their morbidity and mortality, necessarily offer a most sensitive reflection of the social and physical environment in which they find themselves. Indeed, they are the best index of the adaptation of a society and its culture to the contemporary environment. Curiously, to the best of my knowledge, no social or medical historian has fully explored the possibilities opened up by these generalisations, and to this extent the present work is perhaps original. In a short survey of the history of Australian childhood, I have tried to illustrate, if not to demonstrate, the interrelationships implicit in at least the first of the two propositions, to examine the medical aspects against the social and environmental background, to note the influence of social and environmental change on disease and health, and to consider the impact of medical developments on society and its attitudes. With such a holistic concept, it is inevitable that the book is selective rather than comprehensive. I hope chiefly that the approach may stimulate social and medical historians to study more deeply many of the problems and issues upon which the present work touches but lightly. Certainly, there is a plethora of material which I have not exhausted. I hope, too, that it may help to break down the disciplinary barriers which have separated social and medical history. If it is to serve a social as well as a professional purpose, the history of medicine cannot confine itself to technological development, nor can social history afford to ignore its basic sciences of demography and epidemiology. Australia is, or was, a relatively isolated microcosm, in which it is possible to study both medicine and society in remarkable detail over nearly two centuries; I believe that its history is thus of more than merely nationalistic significance.[1] For all these reasons, I trust that the book has wider appeal than to the Australian specialists in child health for whom it was initially planned. Indeed, the paediatrician may be disappointed to discover that it is not a history of paediatrics in Australia; I have refrained from dealing in depth with the technical and scientific advances of recent years, just as I have declined to follow the broader socio-medical issues beyond about 1920. The compensation must lie in seeing the evolution of a specialty as being within a society rather than within a profession.

It has been found impractical, for economic and other reasons, to provide detailed documentation for every statement in the text. The references given for each chapter have been selected because they amplify the treatment of matters raised in the text or because they provide further references to source material; they include studies to which I am particularly indebted. The select bibliography lists works to which I have frequently had recourse on a variety of subjects but it also includes bibliographies which will assist the reader anxious to follow up any aspect in greater depth. Notably in relation to published government documents, I have usually given in the text sufficient information to allow ready identification of other sources. Particular attention may be drawn to the bibliography of paediatric contributions to Australian medical journals to 1900, prepared by Sheila Simpson and Ann Tovell, which is presently appearing in parts in the *Australian Paediatric Journal.* A revised and updated edition of my *Annotated Bibliography of the History of Medicine in Australia* (Sydney, 1957), currently nearing completion, will provide access to a full range of historical studies on child health and welfare in this country.

Perhaps a word should be said on my frequent use of quotations from Australian poetry. These are intended, not to display a superficial erudition beyond my professional expertise, but deliberately to emphasise the point that child health and welfare were constantly on the community conscience. Poets for the most part express themselves better than journalists, and usually after more profound thought; hence my preference for poetry instead of the more conventional technique in social history of referring to newspaper reports. The poetic interest in children is almost an Australian tradition for the earliest reference dates back to the first ode produced by Governor Macquarie's convict 'poet laureate', Michael Massey Robinson, in 1810. As it refers to the establishment of an orphan institution and is pertinent to both the theme and the title of this book it merits quotation:

    For ever be the Hands rever'd
       That yon blest Sanctuary rear'd:
    That bade the little Wanderers come,
       And found a sheltering, happy Home:
    That with maternal Fondness chas'd their Tears,
       And snatch'd from Scenes impure their op'ning Years.

Poetry, medicine and child health all have their environment in common.

BRYAN GANDEVIA

'Cregganduff',
Mount Victoria,
New South Wales.
    2 January 1978

Reference

1. Gandevia, B., 'The medico-historical significance of young and developing countries, illustrated by Australian experience', in *Modern Methods in the History of Medicine,* ed. E. Clarke, London, Athlone Press, 1971: 75.

Acknowledgements

This project arose from discussions initiated by John Beveridge, Professor of Paediatrics in the University of New South Wales and Director of the Prince of Wales Children's Hospital, as to the form of an historical contribution to the international paediatric conference planned to commemorate the opening of the Hospital. I am indebted to him, to the organisers of the conference and to the Boards of Directors of the Prince Henry and Prince of Wales Hospitals Group for their practical support.

I am particularly grateful to Sir Lorimer Dods, Emeritus Professor of Child Health at the University of Sydney, for his advice and encouragement from the beginning, and for his courtesy in contributing the Foreword. I am grateful to him, to Sir Edward Ford, Dr. Frank M. Forster and Professor H.O. Lancaster for generously reading an early draft; errors in the final work are thus unequivocally my responsibility. The appearance of even a draft is a tribute to the dedicated and unremitting labours of Sheila Simpson; her invaluable contribution is beyond due acknowledgement.

Mrs. Simpson and I wish to express our thanks to the staffs of many organisations and to many individuals for their liberal and courteous assistance in a variety of ways. It is not practicable to list them all, but we would especially mention, amongst institutions, the Mitchell Library, Sydney, the Archives Office of Tasmania, the John Oxley Library, Brisbane, the Medical History Library of the Royal Australasian College of Physicians, Sydney, the Biomedical Library of the University of New South Wales and the Medico-Historical Museum of the Victorian Branch of the Australian Medical Association; amongst individuals, Dr. Howard Williams, Dr. Ian Cope, Professor W.B. Macdonald, Miss B. Heagney, Mrs. A. Holster, Mrs. P. Joske, Miss A. Tovell, Mrs. J. Baldwin and Miss M.J. Anthony. We acknowledge with thanks the resources of the Public Record Office, London and the National Library of Australia and the State Library of New South Wales as directing authorities of the Australian Joint Copying Project. We also appreciated many valuable responses to enquiries of senior medical staff of paediatric hospitals and university departments. The Editor of the *Australian Paediatric Journal* kindly allowed reproduction of material previously published in its columns and also accepted for publication the associated bibliography of Australian paediatrics. The illustrations were thoughtfully prepared by the Department of Medical Illustration, University of New South Wales. Mr. Bruce Semler, of Charter Books Pty. Ltd., has greatly assisted me in the practical aspects of publication.

This work forms part of a more comprehensive project which is supported by the Australian Research Grants Committee.

B.G.

Contents

1 BOUND FOR BOTANY BAY

... a voyage which, before it was undertaken,
the mind hardly dared to contemplate, and on
which it was impossible to reflect without some
apprehensions as to its completion.

> David Collins, *An Account of the*
> *English Colony in New South*
> *Wales,* 1798

Of the two ways by which a European child might arrive in
Australia, the long sea voyage was certainly the more protracted
and probably the more distressing for both mother and child. The
First Fleet set sail in the middle of May 1787, and for most of the
convicts this meant not setting foot on land until the end of January
1788. The fleet comprised approximately 250 civil staff, officers and
men of the marines, 600 male convicts and 200 female convicts;
there were 19 wives with the marines and 17 wives with the convicts.
Thirty-six children disembarked at Sydney Cove, of whom 18 had
been christened on the voyage out, so that a modest number of
births may be assumed. Some two years later, the *Lady Juliana,*
with 226 female convicts, took nearly eleven months to reach
Sydney with 12 children, several of whom had been born on board
with only one death. The female transports tended to make rather
more leisurely trips to Port Jackson than the male transports, and
their arrival was commonly followed by an epidemic of births. The
steward on the *Lady Juliana* observed that 'every man on board
took a wife from among the convicts, they nothing loath'. Even with
the advent of naval surgeons-superintendent in the later years of
transportation, prostitution on board the ships was never fully
controlled. The absence of reluctance on the part of the ladies can
often be explained by their miserable state when put on board,
sometimes naked and dirty, and by the convicts' crowded,
unsavoury living conditions. Nonetheless, the mortality amongst the
women was remarkably good throughout the period of
transportation, and consistently superior to that of the males.
Omitting 246 women who perished tragically in two shipwrecks,
female mortality between 1788 and 1800 was about 3.5% of those
embarked, falling in the next decade to 2.3%, and to about 1%

thereafter; the respective figures for males, relatively few of whom drowned, were 12%, 5% and 2%. The acceptance of an inevitable mortality is apparent in the casual comment of one female convict who came out with 95 of her fallen sisters on the *Britannia* in 1798 that 'on our passage we buried only two women and two children', the number of children embarked being unknown.

The children who accompanied these women, or were born to them on the outward voyage, received scant administrative attention; official returns commonly list 'women and children' together. In 1793, Richard Kent, surgeon to the *Boddingtons,* was obliged to seek official permission to victual some convict children on board the transport 'as I have no instructions about convicts' children'. The number of births on the *Lady Juliana* would appear to have been at least 10, according to Surgeon Alley, and not 5 or 6 as reported elsewhere. The casual approach to the children may be illustrated further in a letter from Governor Macquarie to England in June 1815, reporting the arrival of the *Northampton* with '106 Female Convicts, and 30 Free Women, Wives of Convicts, with 42 Children. Many of these female Convicts have also brought Children out with them', but how many they brought was beneath official notice.

Nearly 25,000 potential mothers of the first Australian generation were transported during the convict era. About half were of Irish origin, 40% English and 10% Scottish; the proportion of English was higher in the earlier years. For example, prior to 1810 nearly 40% of the women came from London, and almost all came from an urban background. Their marital status is difficult to define but half of them claimed to be single, while a quarter of them did not reply to the question. About 45% were aged between 20 and 29 years, 15% were less than 20, and 16% were in their fourth decade, an age distribution similar to that of the males. Over 80% had been convicted of offences against property, and about 60% had had previous convictions, especially amongst the English and Scottish. A high proportion, probably more than the conventional estimate of 20%, were prostitutes; a convict bard, referring to the qualifications of his colleagues to play Macbeth, wrote 'our females have been us'd at night to walk'. Considering their backgrounds, which of course were part of the social state of Britain at the time, and the records of the trials, it is no overstatement that 'one is left with the impression of an indifferent class of women'; almost all contemporary observers, including the surgeons, condemned the ladies in stronger terms. Even Lady Jane Franklin, deploring the system whereby women were transported, considered it 'waste time and labour' to try to reform them. Very few could read or write (15% in two randomly selected transports). Despite the gloomy overall picture, there were instances of injustice and of convictions of women of higher standards for an isolated fall from grace, whilst at this period many who admitted to being 'on the town' may have been led to this profession from better backgrounds through various misfortunes.

For reasons already given it is doubtful whether any valid estimate can be made of the number of children who came to Australia accompanying convict mothers, or with the wives of convicts, whose families were for some years given passages to Australia. It is also not possible to assess the number of children arriving in the first decades of settlement in the families of civil and military personnel, most of whom probably returned to Britain. About 20% of the convicts themselves were aged less than 20 years; from 1788 to 1853 they numbered around 35,000, including 7000 girls. It is a fair estimate that about 60% of the juveniles were aged 14 to 16 years inclusive, whilst 10% of the boys, and less than 1% of the girls, were aged 13 or less. In addition, a small number of 'juvenile emigrants' was sent to Western Australia; they were boys from English prisons who were not to be regarded as convicts but rather as having served their time. Some of the characteristics of the convict youth are reviewed in Chapter 6.

By modern standards, conditions of transportation were most unsatisfactory, both physically and from the penal viewpoint. Where juvenile offenders were not separated from the mature convicts there was intercourse of both a socially and a physically degrading kind, so that in due course more effective means of separation were introduced, culminating in the use of separate ships. Over 2000 boys were transported thus between 1829 and 1843, but the remainder, as well as the girls, were sent out in company with their elders and betters in crime and vice. Among these juvenile ships was the *Hindostan,* which brought 200 boys to Hobart in 1841 under the care of an enlightened and enthusiastic surgeon-superintendent, Andrew Henderson, in the course of his eighth voyage in this capacity. There was negligible disease, and no mortality; careful attention was paid to shipboard hygiene, and a well-organised program of education was conducted — 40% of the boys did not know the alphabet. In the best traditions of the surgeons-superintendent, Henderson also took care of the moral and religious instruction of his charges. On the *Lord Goderich* (1841), surgeon James Baird complained of the want of towels; it was difficult to prevent the spread of ophthalmia, and washing the face in salt water was not ideal. Alexander Nesbit, another highly experienced surgeon, brought out juvenile offenders on the *Frances Charlotte* (1837). He made an effort to educate the youths; examinations were held and prizes awarded. While one-third of the boys were at school, the others were on deck playing games, and dancing was also permitted. It seems that the juvenile ships were one of the more constructive experiments of the convict era. Under these enlightened conditions of transportation, there might have been a place for the idea, seriously put forward in 1831, that convicted girls of 10 or 12 should be sent to school in New South Wales rather than to the penitentiary at Millbank, and that convict boys might well be offered the opportunity to go abroad voluntarily 'if enlisted into a corps of labourers, artificers, or apprentices'.

For the innocent children accompanying their wayward mothers, a voyage on a convict transport was scarcely an environment conducive to the best of upbringing. Not only were the 'tween decks overcrowded by even contemporary standards, but the heat, humidity and stench of the insanitary accommodation must have become unbearable in the tropical nights with the hatches closed, a precaution often necessary on the female ships to prevent intercourse between the women and the guards or seamen. For various reasons, these precautions tended to be ineffective, and there were often occasions when the seamen 'got to the women', to use a contemporary phrase. Liquor mysteriously found its way below decks and vicious fights between the ladies were not uncommon. Once the novelty of sea, sky, flying fish, albatrosses and possibly an occasional whale or an iceberg had worn off, the restricted hours on a deck crowded with stores could scarcely have offered a child much amusement. Commonly, the sleeping berths were arranged in two rows, one above the other, on each side of the ship, each berth being about six feet square and intended to hold four convicts. Light and air were admitted through gratings over the hatches, which were closed in bad weather. Ventilation was widely regarded as unsatisfactory, in spite of regulations requiring the use of various ventilatory aids. All too frequently the ships were damp, or unexpected seas crashed through the gratings; bad weather might confine the convicts below decks for days on end. There were no amenities for children, being administratively non-existent, and no special concessions were usually made in relation to diet. Water was severely limited and many mothers must have had to share their rations with the children.

The greatest administrative advance in the history of convict transportation was the investment of the surgeons-superintendent with considerable supervisory powers and responsibilities in relation to the moral and physical welfare, as well as the health, of the convicts. This measure followed the historic report on the unhygienic conditions of transportation prepared at the instigation of Governor Lachlan Macquarie by the emancipist surgeon William Redfern in 1814. Thereafter, naval surgeons, imbued with the high standards of nautical medicine established by Lind, Blane and Trotter in the eighteenth century, controlled many of the earlier abuses, ensured good hygiene practices and delivered sound medical care, often taking an obvious pride in a healthy voyage.

The journals of these surgeons on female convict ships deserve systematic study for the light that they would throw on contemporary paediatric problems and their management. In later decades these reports took a standard form, and included standardized returns from which useful statistical information may be derived. Even as late as 1843 there were voyages with high childhood mortality; on one occasion 12 children died, chiefly from marasmus, and allegedly owing to the carelessness of the mothers and their bad constitutions. Common diseases were diarrhoea, ophthalmia and convulsions, but many other disorders are recorded and some case histories are given in considerable and challenging detail. On the *John Bull* (1822), following the discovery of a seaman with smallpox, 9 children aged from 6 months to 9 years were vaccinated; the course of the lesions is described in detail and the surgeon, William Elyard, punctured the vesicle on the arm of Elizabeth Wade, aged 2 years 'and took what lymph I could from it, this child being the most healthy and free from blemish'. After two months, during which the progress of the vaccinial lesions is fully described, the surgeon was able to certify that the children had 'regularly gone thru' the progress of vaccination as laid down in the directions'. When one child became severely ill and was admitted to hospital Elyard also admitted the mother, 'to attend and nurse him'. Before sailing, Elyard managed to acquire some children's books, and a dozen spelling books. When he noticed that the mothers were inattentive in giving the children their lessons with the books and cards issued, many of which had been destroyed, he appointed a schoolmistress for the children, and arranged a school for any adults wishing to be taught. Elyard was obliged to exercise his authority in regard to punishment on several occasions; he confined two women to the coal hole for insolence and quarrelling, and he also made use of the hospital to imprison two ladies who had proved quarrelsome — for one who had twice assaulted another prisoner he added an iron collar on her neck.

The following extract from the journal of Allan McLaren, surgeon-superintendent of the female convict ship *Hydery* (1832) reflects concern about another recurrent problem (the same complaint had been made in 1829):

The quality of the provisions at present allowed the Infant in arms is the same as that which is allowed the mother with the exception of Tea — as it cannot be supposed that a child under a year old can digest salt beef and pork, I beg leave to suggest that a quantity of Rice be put on board to be substituted for the Salt provision at the discretion of the Surgeon-Superintendent which would in my opinion be both cheaper and better — this alteration in diet might also be extended to such of the Female prisoners as are 'delicate'. There is plenty, indeed too much, Oatmeal now allowed but when old, as it generally is when shipped, it is so full of insects and so acrid that I could hardly get the English children to eat it and when they did it generally disordered the bowels and stomach and frequently produced flatus and diarrhoea — one half of the oatmeal, allowed both to mother and child might with propriety be discontinued. The present quantity of Pease now issued is more than can be consumed and might be reduced one third... At present it is the practice to embark female convicts that have children so soon as the babe is weaned ... it frequently happens that the infant is prematurely taken from the breast and sent on board before it has recovered the effects of the change and just at the time of life that it begins teething; nor is the mother at this time in a very fit state for embarkation having not yet recovered her periodical returns. The consequence of this is that when at sea on salt provisions the mother not thinking the provisions suited to her infant again puts it to the breast which still retains the milk but *now* of so acrid and alkaline a quality as to disagree with the child and bring on bowel complaints. If it could be done conveniently it would be better to retain the mother in Jail until the child is

18 months. If this cannot be done I would suggest that they might be sent while the child is nursing if three months old.

Dr. McLaren gives a graphic account of other circumstances unfavourable to the health and welfare of the children and babies on board the transports.

But in getting rid of one evil ['cholera'] room was made for a succeeding one of a very disgusting although not very dangerous nature — sea sickness. On getting under weigh the weather proved rather wet and very squally ... the lower deck ports ... leaked very much; as might be expected with such a freight [this] made the prison notwithstanding all our efforts, for the time, in a most horrid state of wet and filth as almost every woman was confined to bed and constantly vomiting. But on leaving the land a fair wind and fine weather allowed almost all to come on deck. The bedding was thoroughly dried, the lower deck completely cleaned and we got rid of such a scum as I hope never to witness again.

It is appropriate to conclude on a rather sad note with a quotation from surgeon-superintendent James McTernan, *Sir Charles Forbes* (1827).

The case of tetanus was a little girl (free) whose mind from the day of our sailing suffered from nostalgic depression and she had repeatedly begged me to let her go home again — she had had a pneumonic attack accompanied by a good deal of spasmodic irritation and it may be called a singular instance of delicacy and sensibility in a creature of her age and condition that I frequently found her on her own and in tears for the misconduct of her mother who was then on board in advanced pregnancy, though her husband had been five years a convict and in Van Diemen's Land.

References and further reading

Bateson, C. *The Convict Ships 1787-1868.* 2nd ed., Glasgow, 1969.
Public Record Office, London. Medical Department. Medical Journals. *Hydery* Adm. 101/35 (AJCP 3198), *John Bull* Adm. 101/38 (AJCP 3199) and *Sir Charles Forbes* Adm. 101/67 (AJCP 3210). Mitchell Library.
Robson, L.L. *The convict settlers of Australia.* Melbourne, 1965.
Shaw, A.G.L. *Convicts and the colonies.* London, 1966.

2 'A WONDERFULL COUNTREY FOR TO HAVE CHILDREN IN'*

So, Australasia, may thy exiled band
Spread their young myriads o'er thy lonely land
Till village spires and crowded cities rise.

W. C. Wentworth, *Australasia,* 1823

In the early years of Australian history childbirth seems to have been accepted as a fact, or hazard, of life, and with minor reservations, there are no detailed medical accounts of difficult labour or maternal death. Three mothers, in relation to almost 250 births, died in childbirth during the first five years of settlement; their three children died at the age of 3 days, 7 weeks and 3 months. Yet, within a decade or two, there had arisen a myth of human fertility associated with migration of the European female to the antipodes. The same idea was expressed by observers of the Californian scene, and it seems likely that the same explanation of apparently enhanced fecundity and fertility applies to both areas of colonisation. Careful examination of the Australian data on births, which is reasonably reliable for the first few years of settlement, and for the female population, indicate that the annual natality rate lay between 15 and 20 per 100 women of childbearing age. As the period was characterised by a gross excess of young males, by considerable advantages in the position of a mistress, if not a wife, and by a concept of chastity on the part of the females which Judge Advocate Collins noted 'had never been . . . rigid', it seems that a birth rate of this order may reasonably be regarded as low compared to an annual natality rate in New South Wales in 1861 of 34. Put another way, the annual birth rate for the early settlement probably did not exceed 25 per 1000 in terms of a standard population, whereas in both Britain and Australia a figure of 35 per 1000 was common later in the century, with a peak of 40 per 1000 in New South Wales in the early 1860s. The conclusion is inescapable that the impression of enhanced fertility amongst the early Australian ladies is not accounted for by a remarkably high number of births. By contrast, malnutrition and gonorrhoea were ever-present reasons for

---

* Margaret Catchpole, a convict midwife, 1807.

impaired fertility in this period. In spite of several contemporary lay and even medical observations concerning childbirth in women beyond the childbearing age, no specific instance has been identified of a child being born to a woman aged over 44 years. There is certainly no evidence for the statement of one visiting medical gentleman that 'almost every woman, under 42 years of age, on her arrival in New South Wales, and properly treated [*sic*], will beget a large family, producing for a considerable period, a child once a year'. There is evidence only that they received the proper treatment. It was a rare instance of *naiveté* on the part of Commissioner J.T. Bigge, appointed to inquire into the state of the colony of New South Wales, when he commented on the number of women accompanied by 'fine and healthy children, some of whom have been born after their mothers had attained the age of 45'. Bigge's comment was based on observing a general muster of the population; there may well have been good reasons for an old lady to appear with a child or two.

A more significant factor than the birth rate or fertile grandmothers in contributing to the subjective impression of enhanced fertility was a low death rate amongst the children, particularly amongst infants. Although the deaths are reasonably well-documented for the first five years of the settlement, there are difficulties in estimating the childhood population and its age distribution at any point in time. However, deaths of infants aged 2 months or less amounted to no more than 10% of the births over this period, and of infants 12 months or less to approximately 20%. There is some evidence of adaptation to the new environment in that the child deaths tended to decline over the first few years, suggesting an improvement in child care or welfare; this would have been more apparent if diseases primarily of adults had not begun to contribute to the deaths of older children in 1792. In other years, mortality was largely confined to infants aged 6 months or less. These mortality rates compare more than favourably with those of London and English towns in the nineteenth century.

The most important contribution to the impression of enhanced fertility was made by the rapid change in the age distribution of the population. The great majority of the population was aged between 20 and 35 years in 1788, with males outnumbering females by approximately 3 to 1. In the whole settlement of some 1500 souls less than 40 were children. In 1792, with a population of about 3000, with the same adult age distribution but with a 6:1 excess of males, there were 200 children. The proportion of children to females had changed from approximately 1:10 to 1:3.5. By 1795 the ratio was 2:1 and it reached 1:1 in 1799, in spite of an increase in the female population. Put another way, the proportion of children, most of whom would have been less than 2 or 3 years old, rose at Port Jackson from about 4% of the total population in 1795 to about 17% (mostly aged less than 10 years) in 1799. Such a rapid change, producing a population with an age constitution quite unfamiliar to any European observer, would create the impression of remarkable fertility. The fact that probably 90% of the women still remained within the childbearing age range might easily escape notice in a period when no population contained a high proportion of elderly people. Such an observer, particularly one of moralistic tendency, might also find support for the idea of enhanced fertility in the low marriage rage (about 2% of single women per annum at its lowest level, between 1798 and 1802), the high illegitimacy rate (in the early 1800s two-thirds of all children were illegitimate), and an increasing number of orphans and abandoned children leading vagrant lives.

In 1810 there was slightly more than one child to each of about 2,200 females of childbearing age, both convict and free, but by 1821 there were two children for each of about 3,500 free women and 1,200 convict females. At both periods the children comprised about 25% of the total population. These figures are interesting insofar as the female population is concerned, because up to 1810 2,600 women had been sent to New South Wales, implying that many must have returned to England or died. By 1821 the total number of women in the colony was approximately the same as the number transported up to 1820, and as by this time many women had arrived as migrants or as the free wives of convicts and other personnel, there must have been a greater opportunity for the women to get away from the colony than is generally conceded; their mortality was never high. These changes were accompanied by some inward and outward flow of children which cannot now be estimated.

It is particularly unfortunate that the records of births and deaths for two or three decades from 1792 are unreliable. More information might be gleaned from studies of musters and other sources, but accurate data for births, deaths, population and age distribution are lacking until censuses commenced after the colonies acquired their political independence in the second half of the nineteenth century. At the close of the convict era, E.S. Hall's analysis of data collected in Hobart confirmed the earlier trends in . that he could point to a child mortality rate (excluding the orphan schools) less than half that of London, and also to a relatively high birth rate; as a result there was a high proportion of children to adults in the early 1850s. Dr. W. Milligan's observation in 1836 that in the formative years of Western Australian settlement 'the children thrive remarkably' is a fair generalisation of Australian experience.

References and further reading

Gandevia, B. & Forster, F.M.C. Fecundity in early New South Wales: an evaluation of Australian and Californian experience. *Bulletin of the New York Academy of Medicine,* 1974, 1:108; reprinted in *Essays on the History of Medicine,* ed. S. Jarcho, New York Academy of Medicine, 1976:158.

3 THE FEMALE FACTORIES AS PAEDIATRIC INSTITUTIONS

Yea, he who looks may clearly trace
  Behind the Sirens' charms
The radiant mothers of the race
  With babies in their arms.

Bernard O'Dowd, *The Sirens,* 1907

No hospital facilities existed for the care of women in childbirth in the early stages of all the Australian colonies, and even the most difficult deliveries were carried out in whatever structure the mother might have for a home, a generalisation which is true for all social classes. For the lowest and most under-privileged of female convicts, namely those who were pregnant but unmarried, the Female Factory became the institution which accepted responsibility for care before, during and after the birth of the child. These factories therefore became not only the first obstetrical hospitals but also the first paediatric institutions, although these medical functions were far from the primary objectives in their establishment. They were usually founded to house the females who for some reason could not be assigned for service, and to provide them with some useful means of occupying their time. The factories necessarily became places to which unsatisfactory and recalcitrant assigned servants, a group which included those who became pregnant, could be returned, and hence they also acquired a penal function as houses of correction. The performance of these complex roles taxed the ingenuity of their administrators and supervisors; they were also sorely troubled by the unrepentant and even rebellious behaviour of the women themselves.

Lady Franklin, writing in 1841 to Elizabeth Fry on the problems posed by the convict females, pointed to a related difficulty, the lack of suitably qualified 'free' people to act as supervisors; if any of the five free men and women employed to look after some 400 women at the Hobart factory left she could see no hope of replacing them.

Major female factories were established at Parramatta (*c.* 1805), Hobart and Moreton Bay (both *c.* 1827), but there were subsidiary establishments at Launceston and Ross in Tasmania, a temporary one at Bathurst in New South Wales and at other centres where male and female convicts were concentrated. Conditions varied according to place and particularly to period, especially when gross overcrowding occurred. Some information, mostly of a critical character, exists concerning the early years of the Female Factory at Parramatta, but more comprehensive data, sufficient to assess the paediatric aspects, became available for both Parramatta and Hobart in the 1820s.

The year 1825 ended with 226 women and 15 children in residence at Parramatta but an influx of approximately 1,100 women convicts into the colony between 1826 and 1828 increased the number to 737 in 1827. By the end of 1828 there were 537 women and 71 children. Governor Darling's report for this period gives no indication of any deaths, but in the report of the board of management for the half year ended 31 December 1828, 9 deaths are tabulated. Later in the report occurs the startling statement 'the number of deaths, 191, of women belonging to the establishment exceeds by one only those of last half year'; details were set out in the surgeon's report but this was not printed and we have not been able to locate the original. One can only infer that this extraordinary number of deaths, if not an error for 19, contained a considerable number of unfortunate children. The report also indicates that there were no opportunities for the employment of women with children outside the establishment; 'convicts with no idle child' meant the employer saved a ration, as Henry Parkes was later to indicate in one of his poems, and mothers thus had little chance of escape. There were probably 12 births in this period amongst women returned from private service to the factory. Of the 208 women in the first or non-penal class, 6 were advanced in pregnancy and 54 had young children, leaving only 107 as 'available for service' as single women.

In September 1836 the total number of women in the Female Factory at Parramatta was 590, of whom 30 were sick and 108 were nursing children. There were 134 children confined with the women, 68 under 1 year, 32 between 1 and 2 years and 34 between 2 and 3 years; above this age the children were usually transferred to the male and female orphan schools. The weekly average of women in the institution had increased from 441 in 1832, when the number of children was 112. Usually about 60 of the women were nursing infants born to them in the factory, while about 30 of the women were employed to care for the children. About 5% of the women were in hospital and 1% in solitary confinement for their misdeeds.

In 1840 there were 847 women, with 364 children, but then the number of women rose rapidly to 970 in 1841 and a peak of 1,200 in July 1842, because of a diminishing demand for convict servants as a result of drought and increasing maintenance expenses, and also owing to the increased immigration of free women, who were preferred as servants. About 50 women had also been transferred on the closure of the female establishment at Moreton Bay. The number of women in the Factory's hospital remained constant at 25 or so, suggesting that this was the limit of its accommodation. A constant proportion of 15% was in the second class, namely nursing children (the first class was there not as a punishment but because they had not been assigned for one of several reasons), while the third class, comprising about 25%, was under sentence of secondary punishment for offences committed in the colony. The reason for the increased number of children was that formerly they had been removed at 3 years of age to the orphan schools, but these had become so filled with the children of immigrants that it was no longer possible to dispose of the convict children in this way; from one emigrant ship alone 27 children had been sent to the orphan schools! However, from the educational viewpoint, children above 1 year were made to attend an infants' school in the Female Factory. Convict women bringing children with them to the colony were sent direct to the Factory, but most of the new arrivals found their way there within a year, 'not a few of them in a state of pregnancy'. The Governor, Sir George Gipps, was anxious to abolish the assignment of women because of its association with pregnancy, but this was precluded because of the worse overcrowding which it would produce in the Factory.

At Hobart, a Female Factory was established at Cascades in 1827 when a former distillery was converted into a female factory with a hospital and nursery. In 1833, 37% of the children passing through the establishment in a year died, 42% in 1834 and only 14% in 1836, an indication of the effects of epidemic disease. The infant mortality rate was particularly high, probably due to the manner in which the infants were fed and to the food with which they were provided, together with an inadequate supply of lactating mothers with sufficient breast milk to feed another child besides their own. James Backhouse, the Quaker investigator of Australian penal stations, referred to the 'strong temptation to the mothers, to keep their infants in a weakly state, that the time apparently necessary to nurse them at the breast, may be lengthened, and [thus] the time of entering upon their own punishment, may be delayed: as well as to instigate the nurses to neglect their children, in order that it may be needful to bring their mothers back to them', the nurses being also convicts. The *True Colonist,* in the midst of a public outcry in 1838, asked 'What but death or worse than death, an emaciated existence during the whole period which that life may be continued, can result from the weaning a number of children, several by one woman, the food given to all of them at one time, (for it cannot otherwise be provided in a warm condition) so that their little heads are stretched forth towards the feeding spoon which is offered to them in succession'. To obtain food at all was 'an effort of which even the healthiest of infants are either unwilling or incapable'. The children were usually fed on milk, bread and sugar, the sick ones given sago and wine. Even contemporary observers thought the diet inadequate, and it was certainly lacking in protein and vitamin C. The suckling nursery was divided into an upstairs floor and a ground floor, and it was pointed out that all the recent deaths had occurred on the unventilated lower floor. In the children's wards some 'seventy human beings' were confined in two small rooms each about 28 feet by 12 feet. In the weaning room there were 35 children, 'the effluvia from which even in the day time, the Jury found most offensive'. Following these criticisms a separate nursery institution at Dynnyrne was established in 1842 for mothers with children, but several changes of location in the next decade or so effected little improvement.

At one of the several inquiries (1841) into conditions at the Female Factory and its nursery, the matron of the latter, Mrs. Slea, considered the children generally healthy, and went on to provide valuable insights into convict motherhood. She mentioned that assignable women, when directed to take care of the children, disliked the labour so much that they absconded. Mothers at the nursery were employed to look after other children besides their own, and they took great care of both so as to avoid being sent back to the factory. When asked what would be the effect of separating the mothers from their children after weaning, Mrs. Slea observed that the only inducement to conduct themselves well as assigned servants was the hope of being permitted to see their children; there were few who did not conduct themselves as good mothers. The women would consider it a punishment to be taken from their children early so that they could be sent into assignment. The children were kept at the nursery until the age of 2, and then sent to the orphans' school unless the mother took charge of them, which some did upon producing a certificate of good conduct and of ability to support them.

The time of weaning depended largely on the child's state of health but it was usually 9 to 12 months. After the children were weaned the best disposed women were appointed to take charge of them, two children to each, for 6 months, but they were not allowed to remain longer in the institution unless their children were sickly.

The medical officer, Dr. Dermer, drew attention to considerable overcrowding at the nursery and also of the sick at the Factory. The nursery had all but one of its rooms in use both day and night, which he considered disadvantageous. Although the children were 'pretty healthy', the mortality was greater than in his private practice, partly because of poor ventilation but chiefly because many of the children were 'born with diseased constitutions and have no strength to bear up against the bowel complaints which carry them off at the period of teething'. The daily ration, which he thought was good, for the mothers was 1 lb white bread, ¾ lb meat, ¾ lb vegetables and a small supply of tea, sugar, salt and oatmeal. The children, in addition to medical comforts, received at the age of 9 months a ration of 8 oz white bread, 4 oz meat, 8 oz vegetables, 2 oz oatmeal and 1 pint of milk. The most frequent diseases were diarrhoea and convulsions, but the women were generally very healthy.

The Reverend T. Ewing, in charge of the orphan institutions, asked about the health of the children when received from the

Factory, observed that they were 'much more subject to diseases of the worst kind than any of the others, such as marasmus, cancer, &c. During the last year two children aged about two or three years died of venereal disease'. The high mortality at the orphan schools was in fact defended on the grounds that they allegedly acted as an infirmary for the Factory.

Over a two-year period 1852-54 there were 185 newborn among a total of 464 children passing through the care of the nursery. Of these, 224 (48%) had died, but 10% had died of congenital syphilis, a condition for which the institution was not responsible. The Deputy Inspector General of Hospitals, Thomas Atkinson, submitted that the years 1852 and 1853 had been 'sickly seasons' in Hobart generally; both scarlet fever and measles were prevalent, although neither appears as a cause of death. In 1854 an epidemic of influenza affected all the children, and caused 4 deaths. Death from diarrhoea was dismissed as a common occurrence during dentition, whilst 6 other children (3 with congenital syphilis, 1 with marasmus and 1 with spina bifida) would have died 'were they treated in a palace, as they suffered from the sins of their parents'. In the 3 months prior to September 1855 there had been 125 children through the establishment with only 16 deaths (13%). Improved daily dietary scales introduced in 1848 for the nurseries of Van Diemen's Land were given as follows:

From 3 to 9 months of age — bread 6 oz, milk 1 pint, sugar ¾ oz, sago 1 oz

From 9 to 15 months of age — bread 8 oz, flour 4 oz, meat 4 oz, milk 1 pint, sugar ¾ oz, rice 2 oz and some salt

From 15 months upwards (presumably to 2 or 3 years) — bread 12 oz, flour 4 oz, meat 4 oz, vegetables 3 oz, milk 1 pint, sugar ¾ oz, rice 2 oz, salt.

The women at about this period received 1 lb bread, 8 oz meat and 8 oz potatoes or 1 lb cabbage, while nursing mothers had an extra allowance of 1 lb bread and 4 oz meat, 1 pint of milk and ¾ lb vegetables. The meat and vegetables were made into soup, 25 lb of meat being converted to 100 lb of soup. The responsible colonial surgeon drew attention to the fact that the diet was more liberal for the women than obtained in similar institutions in England, while the diet of the children was so liberal that they could not consume it. Some years later the ration scales were radically revised in the face of continuing criticism.

In defending the mortality in the convict nurseries, it was pointed out that 366 deaths among 1,148 children passing through the establishments was only 32%, by comparison with child mortality (expressed as a percentage of total childhood deaths) from a variety of urban populations of about 40%. The comparison is, of course, invalid, in that the child population in the institutions was to some extent 'floating', the entire number of children not being continuously at risk. It might be argued with more cogency that the

TABLE 1

AGE DISTRIBUTION OF DEATHS UNDER 3 YEARS AS A PERCENTAGE OF TOTAL DEATHS IN CONVICT NURSERIES AND IN HOBART 1851–1854

	Convict nurseries	Hobart
Number of deaths	366	1,520
< 1/12*	9.6)	19.1)
1-2/12	8.2)	7.3)
2-3/12	7.1) 37.5	5.2) 43.9
3-6/12	12.6)	12.3)
6-9/12	7.9	9.3
9-12/12	13.1	9.7
1-2 years	29.8	27.2
2-3 years	11.7	9.9
Total < 12/12	58.5	62.9

* Includes 9 stillbirths; stillbirths were not reported in Hobart.

mortality was unsatisfactory because the number of deaths in the institution over a 4-year period exceeded the number of births by about 9%, a quite exceptional event in any 'free' population, although in fact it appeared to occur in 1853 in Hobart generally (where births were under-registered). The age distribution of deaths, expressed as a percentage of the total deaths under 3 years of age, is shown in Table 1, where the data for the convict nurseries are compared with those for Hobart district. A surprising feature is the high mortality amongst Hobart children under the age of 1 month, the figure being almost double that observed in the convict nurseries in the same age group. It is also notable that in both series about 40% of the child deaths took place under the age of 6 months, that is, before weaning would usually have occurred, at least in the convict nurseries. Indeed, the fact that breast feeding was the rule in the nurseries is probably responsible for their slightly better mortality rate during this period. It is difficult to resist the conclusion that a significant proportion of the Hobart children were unwanted even on the charitable hypothesis that Hobart children, by tradition and general acceptance, were weaned almost at birth.

Table 2 shows a comparison of selected causes of death in the convict nurseries and in Hobart district based on figures compiled by Dr. E. Swarbreck Hall for 1851-54. Any conclusions from data with unavoidable limitations must be guarded, but it is interesting that an excess mortality from gastrointestinal disorders appears to be 'replaced' by deaths from convulsions in the Hobart children. Cancrum oris is absent in the latter group, but strangely the nurseries remained free of croup. The annual age-specific mortality rates (0-3 years) were approximately 10% for Hobart district and 30% for the nursery children.

TABLE 2

CAUSES OF DEATH IN CHILDREN UNDER 3 YEARS OF AGE AS
A PERCENTAGE OF TOTAL DEATHS IN CONVICT NURSERIES
AND HOBART DISTRICT, 1851 – 1954

	Convict nurseries	Hobart
Total deaths	366	1,093
Dysentery, diarrhoea, enteritis	51	13
Atrophy, debility, marasmus	13	11
Convulsions	8	20
Influenza	7	4
Bronchitis, pneumonia	6	<1
Cancrum oris	4	0
Prematurely born	3	9
Teething	<1	8
Inflammation of the lungs	<1	8
Croup	0	4

In contradistinction to the views of the matron mentioned above, it was officially stated that the children in the convict nurseries 'were the offspring of vicious parents, that a large proportion [estimated at 10%] ... were diseased from birth, that their mothers were frequently without natural affection for them, some indeed regarding them as the occasion of their punishment, and that in addition to this, their prolonged imprisonment exercised a depressing effect upon their minds'. If these observations are true of the convict women in the factory, then they may have been true of a proportion of the Hobart female population. Only about 5% of births in Hobart were illegitimate, but in many cases the father, if identifiable, would be contributing nothing to family stability or child maintenance. The explanation for the relatively high mortality in the first months of life amongst the Hobart children must remain speculative; perhaps study of infant mortality in non-convict states might throw further light on the problem. Led by Hall, controversy over the welfare of children in the care of the state continued for another 20 years in Tasmania, and there is much further information available than it is feasible to consider here.

The Female Factory at Brisbane was established some time between 1827 and 1829 and continued for rather less than a decade. It probably never had more than 50 female inmates, whilst the child population over this period rose from an average of about 39 to 64. Three childhood deaths are recorded amongst 22 births over 3 years 1832-1835. Of all the female factories, the only one which seems to have earned commendation was that at Ross, where in the early 1850s about 100 women and children were said to be happy and healthy while the institution was under the supervision of Swarbreck Hall.

References and further reading

Brown, J. *Poverty is not a crime: the development of social services in Tasmania 1803-1900.* Hobart, 1972.

Forster, F.M.C. The female factories. *Proceedings of the Medico-Legal Society of Victoria,* 1970-1974, 12: 202.

Hall, E.S. *Causes of death registered at Hobarton of children of three years and under, for years 1851-1855...* Archives Office of Tasmania, N.S. 308/2/1.

Hutchinson, R.C. Mrs. Hutchinson and the female factories of early Australia. *Tasmanian Historical Research Association. Papers and Proceedings,* 1963, 11: 50.

Report of the board of enquiry into prison discipline... 1841-1845. Archives Office of Tasmania, CSO. 22/50.

4 CHILD MORTALITY AND MORBIDITY IN THE FIRST SETTLEMENTS

The breasts ye suck are seared with sin,
  Or sorrow blinds the eyes ye seek!

W.H. Ogilvie, *The Bundle in the Shawl,*
c. 1910

MORTALITY

Information concerning paediatric mortality in the first decades of most settlements is sparse, but some reliable data are available for the first 5 years of the settlement at Sydney Cove. These 'hungry years' were a struggle for survival, but although the colony commonly lived in a state more or less approaching semi-starvation, deaths attributable specifically to this cause were very few relative to the total mortality. This occurred chiefly in three epidemics. The first, early in 1788, was of dysentery and scurvy associated with the establishment of the settlement, and in this the children shared. There were approximately 10 childhood deaths in the first few months out of less than 50 children at risk. The second epidemic was associated with the arrival of the Second Fleet and was confined to the maltreated adults who arrived on it; there was no change in the now established pattern of about 2 child deaths per quarter. A hint of a problem which was to become more important in later years emerged in a slight excess of deaths in the summer of 1789-90, presumably due to 'summer gastroenteritis'. For a year following the arrival of the Third Fleet towards the end of 1791 there prevailed amongst the adult convicts, chiefly the men, a very fatal and curious disorder, virtually confined to the recent Third Fleet arrivals. During this period there were approximately 40 deaths amongst children, and, by comparison to the age distribution of earlier child deaths, a disproportionate number of older children was affected. Although there is little doubt that typhus and typhoid fevers, as well as dysentery, prevailed during this period, it is difficult to assign all the adult deaths to these causes, and the view has been advanced that these deaths were attributable to a psychosocial malaise, born of despair, rejection and a harsh physical and personal environment, or at least that these considerations were responsible for the high case fatality rate. There are no contemporary clinical descriptions which would enable any more specific diagnosis in the children, but it is again curious that a disproportionate number of children of Third Fleet convicts died. Only about 25% of the total childhood deaths in the year-long epidemic had a First Fleet parent, although First Fleet children must have accounted for half the childhood population, and for an even higher proportion of the older children. The relative absence of involvement of the earlier arrivals, adult or child, in this epidemic mortality tends to exclude the usual infectious and contagious disorders, just as it also tends to exclude diseases spread by water, milk, food or flies. Towards the end of 1792, after a declining mortality in winter, there was a significant rise in childhood mortality with the approach of hot weather.

Unfortunately, statistics of morbidity group the women and children together and there is no official record of the complaints of childhood. The only hint of medical treatment for a child is Catherine Prior's statement that she was at the hospital with an infant in her arms on a Sunday afternoon when she was grossly abused by Samuel Barsby; the child died three weeks later. Of the 77 children who died between 1788 and 1792, no evidence as to the cause of death survives from a medically qualified source. One child, age unknown, of a marine sergeant 'died of Fever' in March 1788 and the father died five weeks later of 'fever and flux'. Two children were accidentally drowned, being the only deaths recorded as due to accident or trauma, later to become a significant and continuing cause of childhood mortality. The Reverend Richard Johnson and his wife had a child which was stillborn and one child died from three sets of twins born between 1788 and 1782 to three different couples. As previously mentioned (Chapter 2), the children of all three mothers dying in childbirth also died. The Baughan family lost four children in succession (probably all aged less than 3 months), no two of the children being alive simultaneously.

John Baughan (Bingham), an ex-cabinet maker aged 34 years, 'of a sullen and vindictive disposition' was transported on the *Friendship* in the First Fleet; he married Mary Cleaver, *Charlotte,* on 17 February 1788. Their child, age unknown, was christened on 27 March 1788, and died next day. They had three further children who died in August 1789, September 1790 and December 1791; two, probably all three, were aged less than 3 months. The burial of the second child took place on 27 August 1789; on 29 August John Baughan was found guilty of causing a disturbance on the night of 26 August 1789 and sentenced to 50 lashes; he admitted to striking his wife with his fist and she had cried out 'murder' several times. When his sentence expired in 1791 he became a settler at Parramatta and Prospect Hill. By 1796 he had a small land grant on the waterfront on the east side of Sydney Cove, he was employed as a master carpenter and he had been involved in a serious dispute with ex-convict members of the New South Wales Corps. There is no evidence that any of the children's deaths were other than natural, although it is a surprisingly high mortality for one family in that period.

Except possibly for this strange family history, we have found no direct evidence of infanticide, nor, incidentally, of abortion. Thus, beyond diarrhoea, dysentery, scurvy, 'fever' and accidental trauma, no authenticated medical diagnostic labels can be attached to any of the childhood deaths.

Throughout the colonial period from Phillip to the later governors, and especially Macquarie, the convict women were regarded as a poor source of labour, chiefly because they had to devote themselves to their children. Their maternal responsibilities were acknowledged and accepted, if at times reluctantly, by successive governments; the mothers had time to bring up their children in the alien environment, even, according to Lady Franklin, in the environment of Hobart's Female Factory.

If such data as exist for Sydney and Parramatta may be accepted, there were only 204 deaths of children of convicts and military and civil personnel in the years 1793-1800 inclusive. By this time there were about 1,000 children and 1,000 women in the colony, with approximately 110 births per year; child mortality, including no doubt a major contribution from infants, was usually of the order of 20% of the births. In 1795 there were 101 births and only 9 child deaths among a total of 43 deaths at all ages. Although the figures after 1792 must be treated with considerable reserve, the evidence is consistent with the view that childhood mortality continued to be relatively low for perhaps a decade or more into the nineteenth century; except for a little 'summer gastroenteritis', infectious diseases remained absent. This is interesting evidence of adaptation on the part of a penal colony to the environment. By contrast, child deaths accounted for 50% of all deaths (which were not inconsiderable amongst adults) in the early years of settlement in South Australia, where there were no convicts but much dysentery, noted as very fatal to the younger children.

Causes of death are not available for Sydney in its first decades, but are recorded from the earliest years of settlement in Western Australia. A partial tabulation of approximately 300 child deaths (aged 0-6 years), occurring in a total of nearly 1,100 deaths at all ages between the years 1829 and 1855, is shown in Table 3. Although the period covered extends beyond the first pioneering years of settlement, it probably gives a reasonable idea of the causes of mortality prior to the arrival of the infectious diseases; whooping cough was not recorded in these returns until 1850, when 15 deaths occurred. At the opposite end of the period, scurvy was recorded only in 1830, shortly after the foundation of the settlement, just as it was in Sydney and Hobart. The figures surprisingly include data on stillbirths and prematurity, but it is not possible to relate these to the number of births over the relevant period. Between 1842 and 1848 infant mortality ranged between 4% and 10% of the births, and deaths under 3 years between 4% and 15%; English infant mortality, for comparison, was 30% in 1839-1840. In Hobart in the mid-1850s infant mortality was about 16% of births.

Some statistics are available for the final decades of the colonial

TABLE 3

DEATHS 0-6 YEARS IN WESTERN AUSTRALIA 1829–1855
(% total child deaths)

	%
Unknown	16.3
Infantile fever*	12.4
Dysentery	14.7
Birth accidents	2.7
Stillbirths, prematurity	5.5
Congenital malformations**	5.8
Teething	4.7
Thrush	2.4
Marasmus	5.5
Respiratory diseases†	4.2
Accidents††	6.1
Whooping cough (after 1850)	5.8
Scurvy (1830 only)	1.8

* Includes convulsions.
** Includes 17 cases of 'hydrocephalus', probably acquired.
† Includes 6 cases of 'croup'.
†† Includes 8 cases of drowning and 7 of burns and scalds.

era in New South Wales. For 1830-1834 the mortality of children aged 14 years or less was 4 per thousand of total population. Over the next decade (when measles and whooping cough had been introduced) it was nearly 7 per 1,000, decreasing to 5 in 1845-1849. It rose impressively to 8 in the next quinquennium, years of rapidly increasing migration. Expressed in terms of the childhood population at risk, mortality in 1848 was only one-third that of 1836, but the higher level was regained by 1854, when scarlet fever first appeared, and other diseases were probably epidemic in Sydney. Perhaps the most significant feature of the vital statistics is the relative doubling of the child population, which comprised less than 20% of the total in 1836 and about 40% by 1850. This proportion showed only small fluctuations until towards the close of the century, but by the end of the first decade of the present century it had fallen to approximately 30%. The relevance of the age constitution to child mortality is examined in Chapter 15.

As a generalisation, all the remote and rudimentary settlements in Australia probably showed a transient period of high child mortality, but this was neither higher nor more prolonged in the penal colonies than in those founded free of the convict taint. The environment of the different settlements, for all their harshness and unfamiliarity, soon offered a greater chance of survival for the newborn than did London at the same period, thus allowing the childhood population to grow disproportionately within a decade of their establishment.

MORBIDITY

The information on morbidity, although more varied in scope, can rarely be expressed statistically, but it sometimes provides additional insight into the problems of mortality. Foremost in importance was nutritional status, which was less than ideal in all new and remote settlements with the possible exception of Port Phillip. The best data are available for Sydney, which may be taken as illustrative.

Throughout most of the period 1788-1792, starvation cast its awesome shadow over the whole of the settlement. The official ration for children under 2 years was a quarter of the adult ration, for children between 2 and 10 years a half, and those over 10 years two-thirds of the adult issue, nominally comprising 7 lb salt beef (or 4 lb pork), 7 lb flour, 3 pints pease, and 6 oz butter weekly for men. The women's ration was also two-thirds of the male ration. In November 1789, the women's ration did not suffer in the general reduction then imposed: 'Many of them either had children who could very well have eaten their own and part of their mother's ration or they had children at the breast; and although they did not labour, yet their appetites were never so delicate as to have found the full ration too much, had it been issued to them.' The children's rations were also continued unchanged and indeed Phillip had previously recognised that children sometimes required a more generous allowance. At their worst in mid-1790, the weekly adult rations were down to 2½ lb of aged salt pork, 2½ lb flour and 1-2 lb rice, supplemented by what could be derived from disappointingly unproductive gardens, an irregular catch of fish and restricted holdings of livestock, mostly pigs and poultry. This scale applied to all in the colony except children under 18 months who received only 1 lb of salt meat. According to one observer, it was the salt meat which made so many of the children 'very unhealthy'. The low mortality at periods of worst rations is striking, but of course this observation does not exclude a contribution of malnutrition to deaths from other causes during the epidemic periods.

The loss of livestock of various kinds and for various reasons deprived the inhabitants of 'the present benefit of milk, butter and cheese', although a very limited supply of goat's milk may have been available occasionally to the few. The only cereals, other than flour, were rice, usually of very inferior quality, and maize or Indian corn, whilst fresh meat and fish were luxuries which were infrequently available. Vegetables were often scarce and indigenous antiscorbutic plants were neither abundant nor very rich in vitamin C. The only community source of water in Sydney, the small Tank Stream, was inevitably polluted by man and animals, and its supply was threatened during droughts such as those of 1790 and 1791.

The women of the settlement were not very literate, and no account survives of the difficulty of weaning babies or feeding young children in a hot and unfamiliar climate, in poor housing conditions, with very limited dietary resources, an inadequate water supply and a continual shortage of eating and cooking utensils. The

Reverend Samuel Marsden's wife left her well-stocked farm at Parramatta to wean her child in Sydney; it was not her first, and one can only surmise that she wanted the company of some of the 20 or so respectable married ladies in Sydney. The fact that 60% of deaths in children under the age of 2 years at Norfolk Island at this period were attributed to 'teething' provides contemporary evidence to indicate the significance of the weaning period. It is difficult to imagine precisely how this phase was overcome; one can only guess that a 'pap' of cereal, perhaps boiled with some salt meat, would be tied in a rag for the convict child to suck. It is also difficult to see how the child could achieve minimum vitamin requirements by modern standards, especially of vitamin C, even if a reasonable protein intake were achieved. For an infant or young child, caloric requirements could probably be met, although this was probably the major difficulty for adults.

Dysentery (which must include summer diarrhoea, gastroenteritis and probably other disorders) and scurvy were important causes of mortality at all ages and in all new settlements. Scurvy remained a hazard to infant and child for many years, indeed for over a century in artificially fed infants, although it usually declined in adults and older children after a year or two of settlement with the development of gardens. Nonetheless, vegetables were often scarce, even in the more affluent section of society, and in any case vegetables and fruit do not seem to have been items of diet favoured by government authority in Australia or by contemporary writers on paediatrics overseas. In many settlements, certainly the settlement at Sydney Cove, cow's milk was not available in any quantity for 10 or 20 years; possibly a little goat's milk may have been used but there was no asses' milk, as commended by a paediatric authority in the British *Lady's Magazine* in 1793. The frequency of childhood deaths from cancrum oris, aphtha, thrush, ulcerative stomatitis or more simply 'sore mouth' raises the possibility of a nutritional component, a suggestion supported by occasional mention of 'a scorbutic disease of the mouth'. Oral disease of this kind would tend to accentuate any existing nutritional deficiency, especially with contemporary 'invalid' diets.

In 1803, George Caley, the botanist, assessed the vegetable situation in Sydney and Parramatta. Respectable people of means were often 'without vegetables for some months in the year'. Cabbages were widely used and so were potatoes, although these had been 'very bad and stinking' in earlier years. 'Pumpkins and water-melons are much thought of', while amongst the fruits apples, figs and peaches did well. The salt meat was of a quality which would have led to its being 'publickly burnt' in England, a complaint which dates back to the establishment of the colony. The issue of wheat and maize was very inferior and commonly weevil-ridden, and the wheat often contained such a proportion of a noxious weed that people complained of giddiness and visual disturbance after eating it, symptoms which infants may have omitted to mention.

The first diseases which many children had to encounter were syphilis and gonorrhoea. Surgeon Peter Cunningham (1827) considered syphilis to be rare in the settlement at Sydney, although it must have been present, and in Hobart by about 1840 it was considered to cause about 10% of infant deaths. Gonorrhoea was prevalent and must have been responsible for some blindness, although there is no early reference to suggest that this disability was common. Admittedly, a woman named Bella went about soliciting subscriptions allegedly to enable her to pay the surgeon's fee for the cure of her child's blindness; we learn of this through his disclaimer in the *Sydney Gazette* in February 1807. It is, incidentally, in this year that the first advertisement for a wet nurse occurred, as well as the first case of proven infanticide, the baby having been disposed of in the privy.

We may confidently accept the views of many observers that infectious and epidemic diseases (other than dysentery) were absent, although it is interesting to note 'a few colds' as the only illness in Norfolk Island in 1790. The classical infectious diseases usually failed to survive the long sea voyage and even if they arrived the population was too small to facilitate their spread or ensure their continued survival. No doubt the streptococcus was present, and 'erisypelatous lesions' were said to be common in early Sydney, to which dirt and nutritional deficiency probably contributed. It was an epidemic of sore throats in 1803 which produced the first medical contribution to the *Sydney Gazette*. It was signed 'Amicus', and offered sensible, practical advice to those who found it difficult to get early medical attention. There is nothing to provide a more specific diagnosis for the cutaneous eruption with 'violent inflammation' which affected the Sydney population in January 1804, and especially those who partook of alcohol (no small proportion). The contemporary explanation was the hot weather.

Perhaps one of the most troublesome disorders of childhood, to which it was by no means confined, was ophthalmia, a term which included at least two disease entities. The more serious of these was trachoma, which tended to occur throughout Australia at the advancing edge of civilization, and which also assumed epidemic proportions, usually in summer, in most child institutions. The other was a milder disease characterised by inflammation of the eyelids, commonly attributed to the bites of flies or insects. Probably both found poor hygiene and inadequate toilet favourable to their development, and the former was highly infectious under institutional conditions. The condition is first recorded by Collins in April 1794: 'It raged first among the children, but when it got into a house scarcely any person escaped it.' At Moreton Bay it caused 231 admissions to hospital in a total population of about 1,000 in 1828, and it has been estimated that about half the children were afflicted in Brisbane's early colonial years. Hospital admissions were rather less frequent amongst the military personnel than amongst the convicts, a property which this disease shared with dysentery, presumably implying the presence of social and hygienic factors.

Other colonies and institutions suffered similar experiences (Chapter 13).

The first mortal epidemic disease to assault the colony in Sydney was influenza, which killed many of the very young and the very old in 1820, and was again present in 1826. These two epidemics, with characteristic symptoms, are peculiar in that they do not appear to have been part of a world pandemic, as were the Australian epidemics of 1836-1837 and 1847-1848. Australia suffered a further epidemic of its own in 1860, during a period of nearly half a century when influenza did not reach epidemic proportions in Europe, or at least in Britain. There is no generally accepted explanation for this behaviour on the part of the influenza virus, either in its local variations or its transport with remarkable rapidity across oceans in pandemic years. Perhaps there was an animal reservoir from which variants arose; strange mutants would have been expected in the antipodes!

Mumps were epidemic in 1824 and whooping cough probably made its appearance in 1828, proving fatal to a few children but generally having a low case fatality rate. It entered on board a ship in which its prevalence during the voyage was not declared on arrival. 'Epidemic catarrh', possibly influenza, affected many, with a significant infant mortality, in Hobart in 1838.

Most contemporary observers regarded tuberculosis or consumption as uncommon, or even absent. In any case, the differential diagnosis of the various manifestations of tuberculous infection in children could not have been appreciated; 'hydrocephalus' and 'tabes mesenterica' are amongst the contemporary childhood diagnoses which may have implied tuberculosis but which embraced other disorders. The general consensus was that phthisis was rare in adults, and some resultant cases of infantile infection probably occurred. The disease did not become prevalent in Australia for several decades, although long sea voyages to Australia for the betterment of chronic pulmonary conditions became popular very early in the nineteenth century.

If the child survived the teething period, then his greatest hazard as he became mobile was an accident of some kind. Two drownings occurred in the first 5 years at Sydney Cove. In 1789 an accident of a different character is recorded; a child aged 8 was raped by a marine. Instances of sexual assaults on children recur over the years with reasonable consistency; a medical officer related an increase in this offence to the habit of 'unnatural practices' acquired during penal servitude.

Morbidity and mortality from trauma were high at all ages, as might be expected in a pioneering situation, for many decades. A review of the *Sydney Gazette* for the years 1803-1810 reveals an average of 8 accidents to children each year (Table 4) and obviously not all were reported.

Overall, if one substitutes a motor car for a horse, the pattern is not greatly different from that seen today. Play injuries are inevitable, even if the items played with vary. Burns, commonly

TABLE 4

ACCIDENTAL INJURIES TO CHILDREN, SYDNEY 1803–1810

Play injuries (tools, machinery, firearms, glass, spear, etc.)	11
Burns (clothing usually) and scalds	15
Drowning	14
Carriage, cart, horse accidents	9
Attacks by pigs, dog, cow, snake	5
Falling tree	3
Lost in bush	2
Killed by native, overlaid, drug overdosage, fall, 'stifled in pan of ley'	1 each

fatal, were usually due to clothes catching alight from an unattended fire, and scalds to the child's falling into a large domestic utensil left on the floor; both are understandable in the conditions of the time, but the first remains a hazard nearly two centuries later. The case described as 'overlaid' was a typical 'cot death' (similar cases were described in coronial inquiries as deaths by 'visitation of God'). One baby was tragically eaten by a pig which had been presented to the child on the occasion of its baptism, and other accidents were attributed to these animals; nonetheless, driving the pigs to and from 'the woods' (surely an English parent who wrote to the *Sydney Gazette*!) was an accepted childhood task. The drug overdosage occurred in an infant who had been given an extract of poppy head to quieten it, the forerunner of many other deaths from opium teething powders and chlorodyne in later years.

Half of the drownings occurred in wells, and the editor of the *Gazette* waxed eloquent on the responsibility of parents to ensure that wells were covered; the media were no different in those days, and in 1806 he congratulated himself that this kind of accident was decreasing. He also elaborated on the risks to children of unattended fires, or of unattended children with access to fire, and he pointed out in relation to carriage accidents that if one was not an expert, one should not drive after rain.

From other records, we may identify cases of childhood poisoning due to unfamiliar indigenous plants and fish, and no doubt there were occasional attacks by sharks and stinging fish, as well as contacts with toxic plants, which pass unrecorded in a small series. Another missing cause of morbidity is sunstroke, which seems to have been a disease of a later period. Clothing was often at a premium in early settlements, certainly in Sydney, and perhaps this was responsible for a later concept of 'hardening' infants by exposing them to the weather in light clothing. Equally hazardous, so it was authoritatively stated, was failure to ensure that the child's arms, legs and head were covered from the sun; 'heatstroke' may have been a more significant risk.

The biography of one child indicates that the hazards of childhood life were not to be taken lightly. The younger son of the Reverend Mr. Cowper was given an overdose of medicine which left him unconscious for 16 hours, he was seriously injured by a fall when being tossed by the servants in a blanket, he was nearly drowned in a well, he was viciously attacked by a sow, and he suffered an attack of typhoid fever. He was also a victim of a school outbreak of skin disease of the scalp in 1815 which affected about 50 children. Expert medical treatment was unavailing but 'a poor working man' rapidly produced a cure in every instance by burning couch grass over a wood fire, producing smoke and vapour from the grass which he condensed on the blade of a clean axe. This material was then applied with the finger to the sore for a few days with unfailing success. One wonders whether a desire to wash it off was not contributory. Head lice and scabies, and incidentally roundworms, were common afflictions.

The stories of children 'lost in the bush' are legion for virtually the first century of Australian existence, and they still occur today, even amongst supervised groups of bushwalkers. The Reverend Morison wrote feelingly of these tragedies in 1867:

There is something peculiarly distressing and lamentable . . . when children, so helpless and entirely destitute of resources, are lost. . . . It is a source of bitter and poignant grief to the parents, who are almost more deserving of pity than the lost child, as an occurrence of the kind never takes place without the parents taking the blame of negligence on themselves. . . . I officiated at the interment of one child which came to its death in this manner. The grief of the mother was too agonising to admit of description, and it must have been greatly intensified from the fact of the remains having been found only a very short distance from the house.

He pointed out that those in search of lost children are apt to make so much noise that the child is frightened and 'instinctively conceals itself', and he gives an illustration. From the child's point of view this is beautifully depicted by Marcus Clarke in one of his short stories (Pretty Dick), a story with a special poignancy because one of his own children was lost over a cliff near Mount York, in the Blue Mountains. Less than a mile from where these words are written, there is a white cross which marks the point from which the child fell, and also where, according only to legend, the distraught nurse leapt over the cliff after it.

Incidents of this kind were often described in the journalistic style of the day with the utmost pathos. One five-year-old set out from Campbelltown in search of her 'daddy' who had gone to Sydney. She was lost for three days and the search had been given up when she was found by chance by two horsemen in thick scrub on the late Dr. William Redfern's estate. 'Every rag had been torn from the poor little sufferer by the thorns and brambles, and when she first perceived the horse, she was crawling alone bleeding and faint on her hands and knees. She made an effort to spring towards the horseman, but weakness overpowered her, and with her little heart apparently bounding from her bosom, she made an effort to call 'daddy' and sank almost lifeless on the grass. We are happy to state that the little innocent is fast recovering her strength....', but this was by no means the rule.

The hazards of the environment and the way of life became accepted in the Australian outback of the nineteenth century. A.B. Paterson was but one of many to illustrate this:

And hope died out with the daylight, and the darkness brought despair,
God pity the stricken mother, and answer the widow's prayer.

There were indeed 'hours men cannot soothe, and words men cannot say' for the women of the west (G.E. Evans).

References and further reading

Gandevia, B. Socio-medical factors in the evolution of the first settlement at Sydney Cove, 1788-1803. *Journal of the Royal Australian Historical Society,* 1975, 56: 1.

Gandevia, B. & Cobley, J. Mortality at Sydney Cove 1788-1792. *Australian and New Zealand Journal of Medicine,* 1974, 4: 111.

Gandevia, B. & Gandevia, S. Childhood mortality and its social background in the first settlement at Sydney Cove, 1788-1792. *Australian Paediatric Journal,* 1975, 11: 9.

Joske, E.J.P. *Health and hospital: a study of community welfare in Western Australia, 1829-1855.* M.A. thesis, University of Western Australia, 1973.

5 VACCINATION

Until the fogs which hang so dense and heavy
over the mental vision of the benighted classes
shall have been dissipated by the brightening
rays of actual knowledge operating on the female
mind, philanthropy may shed her tears in vain.

F. Campbell, M.D., *Report to New
South Wales Government,* 1867

Variolous matter for use by inoculation was brought out from England in bottles with the First Fleet but it is not known whether this material was ever used. If it was, it may have been the source of the disastrous epidemic of smallpox amongst the Aborigines in 1789. Except for an isolated case in a negro seaman, the epidemic left the settlement unaffected, in spite of the fact that European children visited one of the natives who were unsuccessfully treated in the settlement.

In May 1803, Governor King reported to England that careful inspection of the teats of the colonial cows had revealed no cowpox, and he requested a supply of vaccine matter. However, according to Lieutenant Tuckey of the *Calcutta,* supplies had been sent out on the *Glatton* which had left England in September 1802, and on his own ship, which left in March 1803. Both these attempts were unsuccessful but Tuckey was undisturbed as he was less than enthusiastic about this new procedure. In 1804 supplies were received in Sydney from two sources, one addressed to the Governor and his principal surgeon (Thomas Jamison), and one consigned privately to assistant surgeon John Savage. The first was again unsuccessful but the latter was effective, and the cowpox was soon well established in the settlement. These events led to the publication of the first significant medical paper in the colony, entitled 'General observations on the smallpox' in the *Sydney Gazette* of 14 October 1804 by Jamison. Jamison concluded in language unlikely to meet with the understanding of most of his intended audience that, in view of the reliability and safety of the method, 'should parents delay to embrace the salutory benefit now tendered gratuitiously, and the Vaccine Infection be lost, the most distressing reprehensibility may accrue to them from their remissions in the preservation of their Offspring'.

It is worth reviewing the details of the introduction of the first prophylactic treatment against a virulent and feared disease, especially as it was the first (other than abortive attempts to maintain the purity of the Tank Stream) public health campaign in Australian history, and the most effective up to modern times.

The *Coromandel,* bearing the vaccine, arrived on 6 May 1804. The Governor's supply was from the Royal Jennerian Society whilst Mr. Savage's came from a member of the Medical Council and was put up in a different manner. It was immediately given to some of the orphan children and to several children belonging to the military; according to the *Gazette* of 12 May, one page of which was given up to a description of the Royal Jennerian Society and a tabulated comparative view of the 'natural small pox, inoculated small pox, and inoculated cow pox', including a strong recommendation to parents to take advantage of the opportunity for vaccination. After some misgivings concerning a 'take' amongst the military children, the *Gazette* was able to announce on 3 June 1804 that the cowpox was now fully established. John Harris, surgeon to the New South Wales Corps, formally advised the parents of children belonging to the military that he would vaccinate them at his home on Tuesdays and at his house in Parramatta on Thursdays until further notice. Meanwhile arrangements were made by Jamison for all children whom the parents wished inoculated to attend at the various centres of settlement. By 13 January 1805 over 450 children had been vaccinated, and every attention was being paid to keeping it 'in constant use on a sufficient number of children to prevent the loss of so great an advantage'. Jamison readvertised for children to be inoculated in remote places in December 1805. On 19 January 1806 he addressed a letter to the public in the *Sydney Gazette,* stressing the advantages and the great parental responsibility: 'Let me again impress on your minds the serious tendency of neglecting so favourable an opportunity, as I have formerly tendered you my services, gratuitously; notwithstanding, parents have been so remiss in coming forward with their children, that I now consider it necessary to inform them, that the vaccine virus must be inevitably lost if they do not permit their children to be inoculated'. He was able to report that more than 1,000 children had been inoculated without complications; there were about 1,300 children in the colony. He concluded that if the settlement were visited by smallpox, with a very high mortality, 'I trust the Public will allow, that no reprehensibility can attach to me, as I have used every persuasion and exertion in my power, to carry such a laudable system into effect, as far as my ability extends; — If frustrated by those designed to benefit thereby, I can only lament their obstinacy, and express my sorrow for the injury done their infant families'. One wonders what were his thoughts, and those of the obstinate parents, when in April 1806 the *William Pitt* arrived from England having had smallpox on board, with one child death. The vaccine matter was lost, although not before it was successfully transferred to Norfolk Island in 1804 and thence to Hobart in December 1805; the loss was presumably due, paradoxically, to the success of the campaign. According to one observer, 'all the young children were inoculated ... but ... the virtue has been lost'.

A further supply was received in 1809, and on 16 October William Redfern, the ex-convict surgeon, was able to report to the Lieutenant-Governor that the cowpox had again been successfully established. In the *Gazette* of 22 and 29 October, he stressed its value to the community and indicated his intention to visit the subsidiary settlements in turn. However, he observed that only a small number should be inoculated at any one time in order to ensure that the virus was kept alive in the colony, perhaps an indication as to how the virus was lost previously. He was still vaccinating at the hospital in Sydney in January 1810. The first hint of any anti-vaccination attitude is to be found in the *Gazette* of 20 April 1806, in a report from England on deaths from smallpox at Bath, 'where the lower orders ... continue obstinately to resist the progress of vaccine inoculation'. Redfern had foreseen resistance amongst 'the poorer orders of people, whose ignorance renders them but too susceptible of the greatest and most unfounded prejudices', and he calculated 'upon every support that example and precept can furnish' from the superior ranks of society.

It is convenient here to summarise the subsequent history of vaccination. Later in the century enthusiasm waned, as no significant epidemic had occurred. In 1840 the Governor of New South Wales again warned of the desirability of vaccination, and announced that it would be available *gratis* in all the colony's hospitals. However, His Excellency was 'pleased to direct, that a charge of One Shilling shall be deposited for every child vaccinated, which sum will be returned on the presentation of the child on the next vaccination day' a week later. This was not only to ensure the 'security to the public' but also the continuity of supply. Within the next two decades, vaccination was to become compulsory in all the Australian colonies except New South Wales. Although there were epidemics in Victoria in 1857, 1868-69 and 1872, there was no epidemic in New South Wales until the occurrence of 12 cases in 1877. The influence of the Victorian epidemic of 1857 is seen in the voluntary vaccination rate in Sydney, when a record number of nearly 2,400 vaccinations was performed, 76% in the last quarter of the year. Over 80% of those vaccinated were aged between one month and 5 years. Although this represented a fourfold increase in vaccination compared with 1855, it was estimated that only half of the native-born population of Sydney had been vaccinated, and that the vaccination rate was considerably less than a third of the birth rate. Despite high vaccination rates in years of threat, from 1861 to 1896 the number of vaccinations was only equal to 26% of the births. The possibility that immunity might be lost by the time of puberty was raised by Sydney's medical officer of health, Dr. Greenup, in the 1850s, but this important public health problem was not further evaluated.

Between 1881 and 1885 there were two waves of smallpox in

Sydney, with approximately 44 deaths. Medical pressure, never absent, was intensified, and led to the commendable Sydney reprint, almost in facsimile, of Jenner's *Inquiry into the causes and effects of the variolae vaccinae* (second edition, 1800), in 1884. Nonetheless, in New South Wales it was estimated in 1887 that 80% of children under five years were unvaccinated, whereas in Victoria, where a compulsory vaccination act was passed in 1874, 86% of children born in the colony had been vaccinated by 1887.

Vaccine lymph establishments were established transiently in Sydney in 1847 and more effectively in Melbourne in 1885. With the introduction of compulsory vaccination, 'government vaccinators' were usually appointed, occasionally without regular medical qualifications, according to professional spokesmen. However, vaccination was not always a professional matter, nor the prerogative of the official vaccinators. The humble journal of a farmer's wife in Sale, Victoria, shows that in 1881 her eldest daughter aged about 3 years was vaccinated by the doctor, and that she then vaccinated two other children and herself from the resultant lesion. Possibly the doctor may have initiated this procedure within families to conserve lymph, and to minimise the risk in the arm-to-arm method of transmitting other diseases, notably syphilis.

Dr. Francis Campbell, in a trenchant attack on apathy and prejudice in 1867, drew attention to a problem which was to assume much wider significance in the battle to reduce infant mortality towards the end of the century; his phraseology suggests that he was well aware of even wider implications.

Whence arises that unsightly brood of moral cankers — the biassed judgments of mankind, the moody bigotries, the opinatries, the ineradicable prejudices, the sophistries, the selfish intolerance, the oily falsehoods winding mischievously through all the business of life? ... they are the exuberant growth of *maternal* ignorance; and it is such cacodaemons of the intelligence as these, progenerating still, that become the most deadly and efficient impediments to human progress.... It is only by instructing mothers, that the seeds of sound and useful knowledge and a pure morality can ever be disseminated.... Enlighten thoroughly the maternal mind, and the husband and the children will not remain long in darkness.

Dr. Campbell advocated teaching the schoolgirls logic, verbal expression, the critical interpretation and evaluation of concepts, mathematics (including some algebra) and 'national philosophy' as a proper preparation for worthy motherhood. As a generalisation, his emphasis on education, even if it did not include biology, was ahead of its time.

References and further reading

Cumpston, J.H.L. *History of small-pox in Australia, 1909-1923.* Melbourne, 1923.

Ford, E. Thomas Jamison and the beginning of medical journalism in Australia. *Medical Journal of Australia,* 1954, 2: 624.

Ford, E. The Sydney reprint of Jenner's Inquiry. *Medical Journal of Australia,* 1951, 2: 320.

6 JUVENILE CONVICTS AND EMIGRANTS

THE YOUNG CONVICTS

There was no official recognition of juvenile convicts as a special group for several decades, and indeed the girls, who were rarely less than 14, were never given separate consideration. There are informal references which suggest that successive governors, notably King, tried to arrange for the boys to be apprenticed or to work in situations where they would have the opportunity to learn a skill or trade, if only from older convicts. That youth was easily corrupted by contact with their elders was widely appreciated, but even when Carter's Barracks were established, primarily for boys, in Sydney by Macquarie, the separation from older offenders in the same establishment was ineffectual. Little is known of Carter's Barracks as a juvenile penal institution, although it appears to have been a harsh disciplinary school rather than any kind of reformatory.

Governor George Arthur described one group of convict children arriving in Hobart as 'entirely useless, and generally so mischievous are these corrupt little rogues that they are the dread of every Family'. Shortly afterwards in 1834 he established Point Puer on Tasman's Peninsula near Port Arthur specifically for their reception, education and training. The concept was excellent in principle but its success or otherwise is difficult to evaluate. By 1836 there were 280 inmates, increasing to 375 by 1838. As a comment on their background, only 44% had both parents living, and 10% were orphans. Two-thirds could read on arrival, but only a fifth could write; perhaps half learned to read and write. School learning, as in other schools of the period, was largely oral and based on repetition, but the instruction may have improved with better facilities and more free teachers in later years; in 1839 paper, pens, slates and

The surgeon, at the door of the "surgery", is dispensing a
potent draught to passengers, mostly children, on an emigrant
ship, *c.* 1860. (By courtesy of the Mitchell Library.)

books were in short supply. Less than two hours a day were spent in school and nearly six hours at some form of labour. Training in trades was a privilege which had to be earned; those available included carpentry, timber-cutting, tailoring, shoemaking, baking and cooking, tool-making, boat building, blacksmithing, gardening and bookbinding. As with the industrial schools, there was a significant output of manufactured items, and boy masons from Point Puer cut the stone used in the round security towers and the church at Port Arthur. Trade instructors were usually drawn from the more reliable convicts at Port Arthur. The diet was adequate, including cabbage or potatoes as well as meat and flour, together with 2 oz raisins for Sunday's pudding. Perhaps the major defect of Point Puer was the recording of convictions for essentially schoolboy offences and their formal punishment by a magistrate. In later life, such a 'criminal' record as many of the boys acquired would stand very much to their discredit if convicted again.

Unfortunately, what happened to these boys in subsequent years is unknown, although Hooper believes that the experiment was successful. Point Puer closed in 1849.

For the generality of the transported boys, at least over the age of 13 or 14, the treatment differed little from that of the adults. Their allotted tasks and their rations were the same, and they were flogged as frequently. Often they were punished on the breech rather than the back, as in the case of several boys who feigned illness at Carter's Barracks. On the other hand, William Gates, the Canadian exile, describes the severe flogging on the back of a thirteen-year-old for absconding. He received 36 lashes from a well-built six-foot man: 'It seemed somehow inhuman that a man of this size, a giant almost, should fasten upon the triangle a little boy ... a perfect Lilliputian'. The boy's attempted bravado, which did not survive the first stroke, provoked his flagellator, allegedly contrary to his intention, into using his full strength because the lad was 'so sassy'. Cruelty in the convict era was not confined to the ruling classes.

PHYSICAL CHARACTERISTICS

What manner of child was transported to Australia? Probably even more than their elders, the children and youths came from the underprivileged sections of an urban environment, with all that this entailed in, for example, early nineteenth-century London. For the most part this group was composed of expert and habitual criminals, whether forced by social circumstances and parental neglect, led by evil companions and indulgence in alcohol, or drifting to the least laborious means of earning a living is of little moment. They were a product of their environment and their time. It would be of immense interest to know what became of them in the antipodean environment.

Their lowly social origins are confirmed by a study of their physical characteristics. First of all, the boys were extraordinarily short, even by contemporary British standards. The average height at 13 years of age was 136 cm, rising more or less linearly to 150 cm at age 16 years, and then to 153 and 156 cm at 17 and 18 years; the London boys were even shorter. They were thus some 15 cm shorter than the most favoured classes in England, and 5 cm shorter than a most underprivileged group (measured about three decades later, over which period there is evidence of only a small increase, perhaps 3 cm, in the heights of British children). Some 57 years later, Australian convict youths, presumably an underprivileged group, were about 13 cm taller than their counterparts of 1840. Modern Australian boys at the relevant ages are about 20 cm taller than the convict youths. For comparison, the average height of adult male convicts was 167 cm, and of females 155 cm; often the children would be as tall as their parents by puberty.

Little reliance can be placed on some of the details recorded in the convict indents regarding the shape of the head and face, or features such as chins, mouths and noses. However, about 20% were pock-marked, virtually a defining characteristic of their origins for the rest of their lives, since no child born in Australia would be so scarred. These marks also serve as a reminder that most had survived an extremely high infant mortality, and had had every opportunity to encounter not only the childhood infectious diseases but also typhoid, typhus, relapsing fever, dysentery, tuberculosis and perhaps even cholera.

Towards the end of the convict era, about one-third of the boys and an occasional girl were tattooed, a reflection of their lowly social origins, of their psychological need to belong to a 'fraternity', and of their background as habitual offenders. The tattoos were of a conventional pattern for the times; the anchor was the most common motif (20%) followed by crosses or crucifixes in 11%. Amorous or sexual motifs accounted for only about 10% of all designs. Letters and the common dots across the proximal phalanges of one or both hands were about half as frequent as the more elaborate designs, but these, as well as the more elementary forms of design, were more common on the left hand and arm than on the right, suggesting the practice of self-tattooing. Tattooing is a fascinating sociological phenomenon, and an analysis of the frequency of tattooing in all age groups suggests that it was a 'teenage' fad of those born in the period 1826-1830. As evidence of its social importance, even a few young Jews from East London were tattooed, although tattooing is contrary to religious dictates.

Two-thirds of a small sample of the convict boys had dark eyes with brown or dark-brown hair and black eyebrows; of the remaining one-third with blue or grey eyes, the hair and eyebrows tended to be lighter, but none from either group appears to have been distinctively fair. Most of the boys in this sample had superficial scars, and over a third had minor facial scars or loss of a front tooth, often associated with scars on the hands, no doubt reflecting a competitive and traumatic earlier existence. About 1% had serious visual defects, 3% deformities of limbs (usually post-traumatic) and 1% the scars of burns or scalds. Overall, the prevalence of lesions which might hinder employability in the colony may be assessed at between 3 and 5%, agreeing reasonably well with an estimate, based on similar criteria, of 4 to 7% amongst a sample of adult male convicts. None of the recorded deformities amongst the convict children sampled were suggestive of rickets.

The girls have been less fully studied; there were few under the age of 15 years, and their records are scattered randomly through the indents of the female transports. They also were remarkably short in stature.

The boys appear to have arrived possessing no physical advantages, other than youth, to fit them for survival in an unsympathetic physical and social environment. A responsible official noted the reluctance of potential employers to 'receive boys of so very small a size and delicate in appearance'. In these circumstances, their future, whether assessed in terms of mortality, longevity, fertility, social or material progress, demands investigation as they must provide a sensitive index of European adaptation to a new antipodean world. Their contribution to Australia in the nineteenth century has been more neglected than remembered, a situation perhaps not strange to the boys themselves, for parental neglect doubtless contributed both to their physical appearance and to their transportation.

EMIGRATION

Emigration of 'free' people to Australia became significant in the 1820s and especially so between 1837 and 1842. The next massive wave coincided with the gold discoveries, after which migration declined until the 1880s. Free, unassisted migration was always feasible, but government assistance varied in its regulation and control as well as in the numbers sponsored, the types of emigrants favoured and the finance available; the system was not uniform amongst the several states. Broadly speaking, financial assistance in some form was commonly available to those with a trade or skill, and to their families, during most of the nineteenth century. Although figures are available for the number of migrants, I am not aware of any review which takes particular note of the child arrivals. No doubt the children of the more affluent travelled cabin class, and enjoyed the amenities of the cow and of supplementary foods taken aboard by their parents. Numerous guides to emigrants described what should be taken for use on the voyage and on arrival; these included suggestions on portable foodstuffs, suitable clothing and useful medicines, graded according to the finance available.

There was some official supervision of emigrant ships carrying mostly government or bounty assisted migrants, and although this effected improvements in the conditions of transportation over the years, particularly in relation to health, it was never as comprehensive or effective as in the convict transports. Although presumably more hospitable than a convict ship, the emigrant vessels were a commercial proposition, and the profit motive often led ship owners and masters to provide less in food, space and facilities than might have been anticipated. The surgeons to the emigrant ships were, in general, less well qualified, less experienced and more inclined to alcohol than the surgeons-superintendent, and they never acquired the same authority. On their behalf, it should be noted that they were engaged on unfavourable terms, often without guarantee of a return passage, and their lack of authority and standing made their task difficult. The migrants voiced both appreciation and criticism of their services.

Considerable research would be required to establish the health record of the emigrant ships. It has been stated that 17% of child emigrants died on the voyage to the Australian colonies between 1853 and 1855, the early gold-rush years. In 1857, the overall mortality amongst 20,000 migrants was less than 1%, but the mortality in children was over 2%, chiefly in infants. In 1859, selected at random but regarded as unremarkable, with satisfactory surgeons and an acceptable health record, 4,300 migrants arrived in Sydney, 17% of whom were less than 12 years old. The 49 births were matched by 50 deaths, 14 in infants, 22 in those aged 1 to 7 years and the remainder in 'adults' over 12. Children over 7 years appear to have adapted well. The age distribution highlights the risks to the very young; only 2% were less than a year old, and about 15% were evenly distributed over the ages of 1 to 14 years. It is interesting that although half were over 21, no less than a third were aged between 14 and 21 years. Individual ships varied; one ship to Brisbane lost nearly 10% of its 250 souls, almost all the deaths being in children under seven. These were the years in which scarlet fever, diphtheria and rubella reached Australia, and their migration was facilitated by any shipboard concentration of susceptible children.

Little is known of these child migrants. In 1859, more than half the migrants came from Ireland, a third from England and the rest from Scotland. Less than 2% of the children under 7 could read or write, but one-third could do so at the age of 14; 55% could do so in the older age groups.

Assimilation was probably not a problem to the children of migrant families unless they should be so unfortunate as to lose a parent on the voyage or in their early years in a new country. On the other hand, Caroline Chisholm's remarkable work in bringing young single women to Australia deserves special mention, if only for the care which she took to ensure that they were safely and appropriately placed upon their arrival.

Decades later, organised immigration of juveniles was fostered by philanthropic bodies anxious to take youth from overcrowded England and offer them a new life in a vast and sparsely populated land. K.O. Fairbridge and his wife started their 'farm school' in Western Australia in 1912, later extended to New South Wales and Victoria. By 1955 over 2,000 children had been brought out under the scheme, and 95% ultimately became successfully established in the community. The chief drawback to the plan was that schooling ceased at the age of 14, and the only subsequent training over the next year or two was in farm work for boys and domestic service for girls. Earning a living in the country at 16 with no special skills was not easy nor did it offer attractive prospects. Many joined the drift to the cities, where there was at least the opportunity for evening classes, and many of the 500 or so who joined the services in the second world war gained further training before re-entering civil life. Overall the scheme was judged a success, both by its founders and by the migrants, but limited funds never allowed the extended education and training opportunities which were originally envisaged.

About 2,600 children from Dr. Barnardo's Homes (established in 1868) were sent, mainly to New South Wales, in the three decades after 1921 when the plan commenced. The Big Brother Movement, founded in Sydney in 1925, brought out nearly 4,000 British youths aged 15 to 18 years over the same period. In Victoria, the Northcott Farm, operating on Fairbridge lines, was established in 1937.

Migration following the second world war raised many problems, largely because the parents often came from European countries other than Britain, and frequently from a less sophisticated and educated environment. Not only was there a language barrier but there was cultural conflict, perhaps most significant within families as the new generation acquired Australian ways. Education posed a problem, and ill-health a variety of problems, both for patients and doctors. Perhaps belatedly, these difficulties are being tackled by the development of a range of specialised services, many of which involve paediatric institutions. It is beyond the scope of this study to examine the childhood difficulties of assimilation and adaptation, but attention may reasonably be directed to a field of historical study in which Australian experience is unique in terms of time and of number.

References and further reading

Gandevia, B. Some physical characteristics, including pock marks, tattoos and disabilities, of convict boys transported to Australia from Britain *c.* 1840. *Australian Paediatric Journal,* 1976, 12: 6.
Gandevia, B. A comparison of the heights of boys transported to Australia from England, Scotland and Ireland, *c.* 1840, with later British and Australian developments. *Australian Paediatric Journal,* 1977, 13: 91.
Hooper, F.C. *Prison boys of Port Arthur: a study of the Point Puer Boys' Establishment, Van Diemen's Land, 1834 to 1850.* Melbourne, 1967.
Lempriere, T.J. *The penal settlements of early Van Diemen's Land.* Launceston, 1954.

7 THE FIRST AUSTRALIAN FAMILIES AND THE BEGINNINGS OF SOCIAL WELFARE

Scenes where my playful childhood's thoughtless years
Flew swift away, despite of childhood's tears.

W. C. Wentworth, *Australasia,* 1823

The first settlement was a complex of social contrasts; there were instances of every kind of sin but there is also evidence of the contrary virtue. The difficulty lies in effecting an objective and unemotional assessment which gives due proportion to good and evil, and a synthesis which allows an understanding of the settlement's society and provides an explanation for its actions and behaviour. The question as to how much the stresses and strains of the colony's curious social structure contributed to childhood mortality is not easily assessed, particularly in isolation from its other problems. In the attempts which follow, no moral judgement is intended or implied, for to do so against such a complex social background would be as invalid as it is unwarranted.

Probably between one-half and two-thirds of approximately 250 births in the first five years of the settlement were illegitimate. Of the 77 children who died over the same period, one-third were born to married parents, whilst there was no record of parentage in about 20%. In a comparable series drawn from children who survived, half were born to married parents and there was some record of parentage in all cases. Children born of convict mothers to officers and civil staff were infrequently represented in the deceased children series, perhaps because the gentlemen kept their distance from the female convicts until about 1790, perhaps because paternity was not acknowledged until such events became socially acceptable, or possibly because they provided a stable and healthy environment for the child. The records concerning the children of P.G. King and Surgeon Thomas Arndell suggest that the latter explanation is reasonable. Arndell, who ultimately married his convict mistress, produced several children whom Governor Macquarie later described as admirably brought up. King's children always remained his responsibility during his lifetime. A few other 'family' histories may be quoted to illustrate stability and instability in both married and unmarried couples, and among the convicted and the free; they also illustrate the kind of stresses which were operative in the social and domestic environment.

Thomas, the son of Thomas Armsworth, a marine, and Alice, died of a 'fever' on 24 February 1788, aged 3 months. His father died on 30 April of 'fever and flux'. In April 1790 the widow, who already had two small children, had a third by Cpl. Daniel Standfield, whom she married in October 1791. All accompanied Standfield to Norfolk Island as a 'marine settler' in 1791. In 1794 Standfield joined the New South Wales Corps in Sydney, and he returned to Norfolk Island in this capacity in 1795. There were two further sons by this time.

The death of James Magee, baptised in November 1789, was the first recorded at Rose Hill on 31 January 1790. The convict parents were married in August 1788 when the bride, Eleanor McCabe, *Lady Penrhyn,* was 27. A second child was born in January 1791. Shortly after this Magee's 'extraordinary propriety of conduct' as a convict overseer led to his being established on a farm near Parramatta, on which he made good progress. Eleanor Magee and her infant child were drowned in the Parramatta River in January 1793 whilst returning by boat from a party at Sydney. Magee, also known as Charles Williams, later developed land on the Hawkesbury River.

Joseph Downey was baptised 10 February and died on 29 February 1788. The father is not recorded but the mother was Sarah Bellamy, aged 18 at the time of her arrival in the *Lady Penrhyn.* As she was convicted and imprisoned at the age of 14 it is possible that this was her first child. In August 1789 she complained, unsuccessfully, that she was disturbed in her hut at night by Captain Meredith and Mr. Keltie. In October 1790 she had a child by James Bloodsworth, a convict employed as a gang overseer and later as a master bricklayer, to whose building skills the colony became much indebted. This couple had five children up to 1800, and Bloodsworth was one of the most respected of the ex-convicts at the time of his death in 1804.

John Matthew was also christened on 10 February 1788; the father is not known but the mother was Catherine Prior (Fryer), *Charlotte.* In mid-February, she was at the hospital with the infant in her arms when she was accosted by Samuel Barsby, who said 'You infernal fury, where are you going?', and offered worse threats and abuse, for which offence (and not for the last time) he received 50 lashes. The child was buried on 18 March. In December 1792, she married John Arscott, a convict carpenter pardoned for his role in putting out the fire on the *Sirius* when it was aground at Norfolk Island; perhaps he was justifying his insolent and contemptuous behaviour to some seamen in 1788. The pair embarked for England in 1793 but she died of 'spotted fever', the effect of 'frequent inebriety' en route; he was involved in other remarkable adventures.

Susannah Holmes, *Friendship,* aged 23, married Henry Kable (Cable), a convict labourer aged 21, on 10 February 1788 and a twin son and daughter were christened on 5 December. These two were associated in Norfolk before leaving England, and a previous child, Henry, is recorded as being on the *Friendship* in October 1787. He was 'still living — of a weakly constitution but a fine boy' in July 1788. Other children were baptised in April 1791 and 1793, and there were later additions to the family. Kable became a watchman and in 1794 was granted land near Petersham, presumably for good conduct as his sentence had not expired. He developed extensive trading interests, dying in retirement in 1846; his wife died in 1825.

John Herbert and Deborah Ellen, *Prince of Wales,* both convicts, were married on 2 April 1788. In December she accused her husband of beating her without just cause, but she made a poor witness as she received 25 lashes and was ordered to return to her husband. A son was born in July 1790 and another in December 1791, at Parramatta. In the following month Herbert was established on a farm as Prospect Hill. Further children arrived, in 1795, 1797 and 1800.

The child of Pte. Alexander McDonald and Mary Phillips, *Charlotte,* was christened on 5 September 1789. In November 1788, whilst living with one man, she slept with another, and declined the advances of a third, thus precipitating two fights which led to the death of one suitor. In February 1789 Mary received 25 lashes for baking flour over a fire on an iron spade, an implement then much valued, and at a time of shortage of kitchenware. Although not on the original list of marines intending to become settlers, McDonald seems to have been settled with other ex-marines at Field of Mars in February 1792, and to have married Mary Oliver in the following months. Mary Phillips married John Pye in December 1789.

Nearly 60 family histories, drawn from the families with and without deceased children, have been compiled from a variety of sources, and a review of them allows an interpretation consistent with the figures quoted above, namely, that there was a higher mortality amongst the children of less stable liaisons. Nonetheless, individual family histories also indicate that no generalisation can be accurate; some of the unmarried convicts provided a stable, if at times tumultuous, domestic environment. The women who became pregnant to soldiers or marines on the voyage out were perhaps the most unfortunate, since the seamen returned in a few months and the marines returned as a body in 1791.

A female convict, writing home in November 1788, painted a gloomy, and perhaps rather pessimistic, picture of the ladies' fate. Their distresses were past description, being now deprived of the indulgences offered them by the sailors on the voyage. Those who had young children were wretched, but those who 'became pregnant on the voyage, and are since left by their partners ... are not likely even here to form any fresh connections'. Some of the sailors wanted to stay behind and become settlers to stay with their women but Collins was sceptical as to the significance of these associations. He was also cynical concerning the associations between convict men and women; a projected plan for escape, in his view, would have been betrayed by the women accomplices if they had been bound by any ties of affection to their menfolk 'but not having any interest in their flight, or in their remaining here, they were silent'. On the other hand, Captain Tench, perhaps the most human of all the observers of the early settlement, recorded an occasion when he 'saw several women running to and fro with distracted looks, congratulating each other, and kissing their infants with the most passionate and extravagant marks of fondness'; the occasion was the arrival of a long awaited ship from England, removing, at least temporarily, their feeling of utter isolation from the mother country.

Understandably, this period saw the genesis of major social problems in relation to child welfare. 'Problem families' were recognised by the settlement administration at an early stage. In February 1789, a girl 4 years old was removed from her mother's care to save her from the 'inevitable ruin' which would have been her lot. The mother was 'a woman of abandoned character', and had shortly before been stabbed by the convict with whom she was living. She was charged with stealing a shirt which she said that she had received in return for sleeping with a marine on Christmas Eve, and she also received 25 lashes for abusing a sentinel. Later in the year she was convicted of stealing clothing and provisions. By this time, her child, together with an orphan of convict parentage, had been sent by Governor Phillip to Norfolk Island, there to be taught reading, writing and husbandry. Both children were to be put in the care of a trustworthy person who was to receive additional ground to cultivate for the children's benefit. Collins hoped that these measures, 'in which every friend of humanity seemed to feel an interest' would prove a success. Social considerations probably also led to the transfer of other children to Norfolk Island, such as those of Elizabeth Basin whose 'husband' had returned to England, and the 6 years old William Snaleham. This boy was the son of Elizabeth Needham, most probably by a marine with whom she had cohabited on the *Lady Penrhyn* during the outward voyage. Although she had a husband in England at the time of her conviction in 1786, she married William Snaleham on 17 February 1788, and this child was born in August of the same year. When her third child was born in 1794 William seems to have been sent off to Norfolk Island.

Private John Easty, a marine, recorded on 17 October 1789 that 'Susannerh Allen Departed this Life of Child Berth and Left the infant Bestard'. The child, son of a marine, was christened a week or so later, and two magistrates decided that another convict woman should be allowed to keep the child 'as long as she did justice to it'; there is no evidence that this foster mother had recently had a child of her own. The infant died when aged nearly 4 months.

Whatever criticisms were levelled at the women, censure was not transferred to their children. Both Hunter and Tench, in the early 1790s, agreed that the salubrious climate was responsible for the production of 'as fine, healthy, strong children as ever were seen'. However, with the passage of time, and again in the social circumstances of the colony, it was inevitable that there should be increasing numbers of orphans or of abandoned children; one can only wonder how they survived. The state of the settlement may be gauged from the official statement in 1806 that there were 395 wives in the colony and 1,035 unmarried women, most of whom 'cohabit openly with some man'. Approximately 25% of the children were victualled from the Government Store, an indication not of neglect (many were soldiers' children) but of the amount of state aid required to ensure that the settlement's children were fed. Governor Hunter later deposed before the Select Committee on Transportation (1812) that 'a considerable number of children were born without knowing who was their father'. Later, the fathers of the children were obliged to maintain them, but this was not true of his own period as Governor. Phillip had not overlooked this problem, because on 4 April 1791 he issued a general order to the effect that no one with a child or wife incapable of maintaining themselves would be permitted to quit the colony without leaving sufficient security for their support.

On his return to the colony as Governor in 1797 Hunter does not seem to have been disillusioned by the state of the children. They were 'charming'; he was concerned that they should be victualled from the store even when the convict parents had become free, and he continued to ration the children of the soldiers because the pay of a private soldier could not maintain them.

One of King's earliest impressions as Governor was the number of children (about 400, or 40%) 'abandoned to misery, prostitution and every vice of their parents', although he also observed that 'finer or more neglected children were not to be met with in any part of the world'. His incentive for establishing an orphanage lay in 'the distressing prospect of the rising generation in this colony becoming the inheritors of their abandoned parents' profligate infamy for want of an asylum to withdraw the orphans and other objects from the vile examples they hourly witness'. He referred to his experience on Norfolk Island as showing the potential value of an orphan institution in Sydney; as he had not only his own two illegitimate children born on Norfolk Island but also a number of 'orphans' sent by Phillip, the idea may have been thrust upon him. Coincidentally, the orphan school which he had established on Norfolk Island was at this time in considerable difficulty for lack of reliable people to look after it — the school master, an ex-convict, was in gaol for debt, and a female mistress, probably also a convict, could not be dismissed for lack of any replacement, although behaving 'very ill'. In these difficulties Foveaux, commandant at Norfolk Island, in 1801 reported 'having repeatedly considered the miserable situation of the children at the Orphan School for want of proper attendants ... I beg leave to suggest to Your Excellency the benefit that would arise to them could they be sent to Port Jackson and the money collected on this island for that Institution be also transmitted and added to your Fund'. By January 1802 King had agreed to this request.

King's orphanage was financed in part by fines from any person 'detected in throwing any filth into the Tank stream of fresh water, cleaning fish, washing, erecting pig sties near it, or taking water but at the tanks', one of the earliest Australian public health edicts. The first building soon housed about 100 girls. About three years later, George Caley, the botanist, was lamenting the absence of a similar institution for males and also the need for both male and female orphan schools at Parramatta; he shared the widely expressed view that if the children were not separated from their parents 'it cannot be expected that they are likely to excel in virtue'. The concept of separation from sin as a justification for institutional isolation, strongly supported by Samuel Marsden, J.T. Bigge and others over the next decade or so, was to be negated by the unexpectedly good behaviour of the new generation (Chapter 8).

King's female orphanage set a pattern of joint government and private control of charitable institutions which was to persist, in various modifications, for over a century. The orphanage was conducted by a committee of private citizens in an honorary capacity, and some private subscriptions were raised. On the other hand, the government appointed the committee, subsidised its work and to a large extent controlled its budget. In many variant forms, this pattern of dual, government and private, control dominated institutions concerned with social welfare throughout the nineteenth century. The intricacies of divided or ill-defined responsibilities set the stage for conflict. The bureaucratic response to conflict was usually an inquiry. The first of these occurred in 1826, when Dr. James Bowman and two others were appointed primarily to investigate an epidemic of ophthalmia in the Female Orphan School. The Board recommended fresh water and a clean towel for each child to use when washing, but it also examined the children's proficiency in the catechism and the scriptures, minutely investigated the accounts and examined all aspects of the conduct of the institution. It criticised the diet, the accommodation, the cellars, and the 'nauseous and unwholesome state of the privies'. Although no great strife appears to have ensued in this instance, the possibilities are obvious, and were realised at other places and other times. For many years responsibility for social services was to remain in a state of uneasy compromise.

Governor King spoke favourably of the comparatively few women from the English counties who were transported. They were often well-behaved, and were preferentially sought after by 'the industrious part of the settlers', with whom they married or cohabited. They adapted well to farm work, and separations were uncommon. He took an opposite view of the free women allowed to accompany their convict husbands to Australia. By 1817, Macquarie was concerned about the children who came out with the free wives of convicts, sent to join their husbands. This indulgence he considered most humane, and conducive to improvement in the morals of the husbands, but not one in ten of these families could maintain themselves, so that the expense of victualling the children fell upon the Crown.

Belatedly, official action on behalf of the vagrant boys commenced. Macquarie was impressed by the number of male children 'left entirely destitute of Support and Consequently living in a Miserable State of Poverty and Nakedness'. He established a male orphan institute for the relief, support and education of these 'unhappy, distressed Children'. Macquarie later reported that this was 'a measure of primary importance, likely to prove of incalculable benefit to the moral and Religious habits of the Rising Generation...'. The boys, who soon numbered 80, were taught reading, writing and arithmetic and the elements of the trades. King had not been blind to the boys' difficulties but funds were unavailable; he had compromised by apprenticing the young male convicts on arrival whenever this was possible. What happened to the neglected male children in the interim can only be imagined. Court applications for maintenance of illegitimate children, not surprisingly, were rare, so that in spite of many stable relationships a significant number of mothers must have had the difficult task of supporting themselves and their offspring. By the age of 7 or 8 the boys were doubtless sent to work.

In Hobart, male and female orphan schools were opened in 1828, again governed by a board of management of private citizens but financed from government sources. Over 200 children were in residence by the 1830s. As in Sydney, and as with the female factories, efficient and appropriate supervisors to conduct these schools were difficult to find, so that complaints concerning their administration frequently occurred. The Reverend T. Ewing, in charge of the orphan schools, who considered that the only hope for young children was early and complete separation from their amoral mothers, illustrated one difficulty when he asserted before an inquiry into their conduct that the mothers scarcely ever came to see the children sober, they sometimes brought spirits and they sometimes made the children drunk. There is a pencilled comment in a contemporary hand on the manuscript evidence which appears reasonable: 'Why permit parents in such a state to see their children? Why should not the interview take place under proper observation?'

Again, as in Sydney, those admitted were not all orphans. There were children of unmarried female convicts transferred from the Female Factory, and some were admitted direct from the convict ships. Vagrant children, and children of profligate and worthless parents were taken in. Fatherless children were accepted as a form of relief, while motherless children were admitted, when space allowed, on payment of an annual charge by the father.

Lady Franklin took the conservative view, widely held until the middle of the century, that institutions of this kind were an encouragement to profligacy, especially as the state did not exercise parental rights. Visiting by the mothers was permitted, and so the children became attached to them as the purveyors of pleasures (and vices) from outside. A child, having been maintained and educated by the government, could be claimed whenever the mother wished, provided she was in a position to look after it; children were usually claimed at an age when their services could be of value to the parent. This problem arose in other colonies prior to appropriate legislation; a first step in New South Wales was an act empowering the Governor to bind children as apprentices (1834).

Dr. John Henderson, a somewhat arrogant and narrow-minded

observer of the Australian colonies, stated in 1832 that the boys from the orphan schools were apprenticed more to the convict servants with whom they associated than to their masters, with understandably evil results. He advocated the obligatory marriage of new female convict arrivals, without sight, more or less as a reward for good behaviour on the part of the resident males. Failure to follow this sensible practice meant, in his estimation, the loss of 1,000 children annually to posterity; the basis of his calculation is not clear.

The problems posed by orphans and neglected children were not confined to the penal settlements. From 1841 onwards there were repeated pleas from Port Phillip for the establishment of male and female orphan institutions similar to those at Sydney and Parramatta but these establishments had to await the separation of Victoria from New South Wales. On a higher social plane, there were problems for the educated and well-to-do parents in ensuring an education for their children sufficient 'to support the character of a gentleman'. For several decades, this meant sending the children to England. The Reverend Samuel Marsden, not one to let a little sentiment stand in his way, referred to the departure of his daughter, at the age of 8 years: 'Her mother did not wish to part with her, but I prevailed at length.' The reluctant mother acknowledged her pain and anxiety but observed resignedly that 'this has been a very bad place for children'.

In 1827 a Girls' School of Industry was established in Sydney under the patronage of Lady Darling, wife of the Governor. This was a private charitable venture, aimed at teaching girls to become servants, which persisted for a century. Its early reports suggest that it was managed well and achieved its objectives. The Society for Promoting Christian Knowledge and Benevolence in these Territories and the Neighbouring Islands, the forerunner of the Benevolent Society of New South Wales, was founded in 1813. The Sydney Dispensary commenced operations in 1826, and over 1,000 patients were soon receiving outpatient medical care. By the end of the penal era the beginnings of an organised, if unsystematic, approach to child welfare were in evidence, but the new and inexperienced administrations, preoccupied perhaps with weightier matters, tackled the outstanding problems with some hesitancy and uncertainty.

References and further reading

Gandevia, B. & Gandevia, S. *op. cit.* Chapter 4. Appendix: Family histories (unpublished).

Jungfer, C.C. History of child health and welfare in South Australia 1836-1936 in *Child Health in a Rural Community Part 2: A further report on the work of the Adelaide Hills Children's Health Survey.* Canberra, 1948.

McDonald, D.I. Care of destitute children in Australia. *Medical Journal of Australia,* 1973, 1: 904 and correspondence, Gandevia, B. *Medical Journal of Australia,* 1973, 2: 46.

8 THE RISING GENERATIONS

'God is from these very stones, from the sweepings
of the Jails Hulks and Brothels raising up Children
unto Abraham.'

Rev. Samuel Marsden, on the
occasion of a young man of convict
parentage offering in teaching the
gospel, 1819.

There is probably no issue in Australian history about which there is
so much unanimity as the subject of the first and subsequent
generations of Australians in the nineteenth century. In spite of the
forebodings of the early governors, priests and doctors, as well as
ladies such as Mrs. Samuel Marsden and Lady Franklin, the first
generation of Australians turned out to be remarkably well
behaved, and also possessed of physical characteristics which
distinguished them from their contemporaries in Britain. This
chapter is concerned with Australian youth over a century or more,
but the initial observations were made before 1830, when perhaps
80% of the children born in Australia had at least one convict
parent.

Mention was made in an earlier chapter of the very short
stature of the convict juveniles sent out to New South Wales and
Tasmania. From various sources we have identified 12 of the first
generation for whom heights are available, and all but one lie
several centimetres above the line of height on age for the convict
migrants. The first systematic data collected in Australia relate to
the heights and weights of approximately 230 boys and 210 girls
between the ages of 2½ and 16 years in the orphan schools in
Hobart in 1849. It is not known what proportion of these
underprivileged and neglected children were born in Australia. At 3
years, both boys and girls were just over 81 cm tall on average, and
by 4 years of age they were over 91 cm. Curves drawn from plots of
the mean values parallel the modern tenth percentile for both boys
and girls but about 6 cm below it for the former and 5 cm below it
for the girls; the girls were thus about 3 cm taller than boys from
about the age of 10 years. Comparison of these values with those of
the male convict juveniles, mostly aged 12 and upwards, suggests

that in the underprivileged orphan group the growth pattern was similar. A tabulation of maximum and minimum heights is also given for children of 'respectable' parents as well as children of convicts in the orphan schools. The maximum heights for children of respectable parents lie along the modern fiftieth percentile, and indeed for girls over 10 years the line approaches the ninetieth percentile. Maximum heights for convict orphans lie along the tenth percentile, where, as a reasonable approximation, the minimum heights of respectable children fall; minimum heights for the convict orphans are several centimetres lower again. Values for children of the 'poor, free' class, where given, are intermediate. The figures are consistent with the view already put forward that, with the exception of the waifs and strays constituting the convict orphans, the first generation in Australia grew taller more quickly than its contemporaries in Britain. As the century progressed, the advantage over British children was maintained, but the distinctions between rural and urban and between upper and lower classes became minimal in the Australian population, persisting for longer in Britain (admittedly, Hobart boys and girls were still a little shorter than their Sydney counterparts as late as 1911!). In this respect, the children in Australia came to resemble children in the United States. In a more detailed review, I concluded that there was no doubt 'that the very short convict boys had been overwhelmed by a taller "Australian" youth within about half a century. By the end of the century, social, economic and geographic influences, and even the influence of criminality itself, were becoming less evident in New South Wales, whose boys were taller than their English and Scottish contemporaries. A predominantly environmental influence on these findings is suggested by the observation that differences in height between children of Australian and of migrant (doubtless mostly British) parents were smaller than the differences between British and Australian children.

The weights of the convict orphan boys appear to be reduced more or less in proportion to height; that is to say, some 60 years later the weights for Australian boys were similar at any given height, but heavier at any given age. The situation is similar with the younger girls, but the convict orphan girl aged 11-13 years and about 133 cm tall weighed about 34 kg; a girl of the same height 60 years later would have been a year or two younger and would have weighed only 28.5 kg. Put another way, the weights for both boys and girls in the orphanages were close to the modern tenth percentiles. There were the expected differences according to social class. Dr. E.S. Hall recorded in 1857 that the orphan boys were 'stunted, fat, pot-bellied, dull and inactive', by contrast with the tall, thin boys from boarding school, who were also muscular and smart.

The following paragraphs are drawn from nearly 50 descriptive allusions to the first and early generations of Australians, whose conduct and attitudes evoked considerable comment.

By 1822, it was observed that 'a great proportion of the children of the first settlers are not so addicted to drinking; and ... become useful members of society'. The children born in the colonies and now grown up spoke 'a better language, purer, more harmonious, than is generally the case in most parts of England. The amalgamation of such various dialects assembled together, seems to improve the mode of articulating the words'. The native-born were said to be like the young people of the United States, not only in speaking a 'purer' form of English but also in being tall and slender, but Hood in 1843 noted that there were some 'very fine specimens of our kind to be seen, above the average height, and with well proportioned frame'. The Australian youths were commonly described as 'slender' and for this reason as lacking the 'muscular power' associated with similar proportions in Britain. There was general agreement that they were tall, and of fair complexion, and that they were capable of 'undergoing more fatigue, and are less exhausted by labour' than Europeans. They were usually 'sallow' or, according to Cunningham, reddish-sallow in complexion. Their straight fair hair was uniformly described, probably as an effect of the sun, for one more careful observer noted that it went dark after puberty. This is likely in that very few true blondes arrived with the convicts; their eyes were usually brown or black. Observers described them as good-looking, and one convict (Mortlock) thought that they had beautiful faces, especially considering their origin from people of 'repulsive countenance'. Both male and female native-born were about 10 cm taller than their convict parents, as indicated in figures given from the Deputy Inspector of Hospitals, Donald McLeod, in 1830, a finding borne out by other data reviewed in the present survey.

Commissioner Bigge said that the young Australians had quick tempers but were not vindictive, were active in their habits but awkward in their movements. With John Macarthur and the Reverend Samuel Marsden, he conceded that they had not the vices of their parents. The relative absence of crime amongst the native-born was finally established in 1840 by Judge Burton from a careful analysis of criminal statistics. Even a critical reviewer of Surgeon Cunningham's books agreed that those of the lower orders born in the colony were remarkable for their good moral conduct. The Reverend Youl judged them more moral than their parents on the grounds that they tended to marry (although rarely with convict girls).

The rapidity of growth in the children, 'with early development of the physical as well as intellectual powers', was occasionally associated with the suggestion of early or premature decay. 'The girl of 15 possessing all the charms, and many of the graces of womanhood, must at the age of thirty, yield the palm to her, who, realizing the triumphs of her sex at a later, preserves them to a more advanced, period of life.' Hood had not seen 'what I should call a fine woman' amongst the currency lasses. The girls were of somewhat amazonian proportions with 'regular, but inexpressive features, rather delicately modelled' but he preferred his ladies on a more modest scale. Mrs. Charles Meredith noted that the children were good-looking when young but showed precocity of growth and premature decay. They grew up tall, 'the girls often very pretty and delicate-looking whilst young (although very often disfigured by bad teeth); but I have seen women of twenty-five or thirty, whose age.I should have guessed to be fifty at least.' She thought the boys too often had round shoulders and a narrow chest, and 'what puzzles me exceedingly ... a very large proportion of both male and female natives *snuffle* dreadfully; just the same nasal twang as many Americans have'; English-born children did not acquire the snuffle or the nasal twang. George Suttor contrasted the lost good looks of the British-born girls, due to liquor and salt provisions, with 'new and beautiful characters ... particularly among the feminine youths of Australia', who were an honour to their race.

The younger generation Australian was admired for his independence and resourcefulness, perhaps because by the age of 8 he was often remarkably knowledgable about running a station or a farm. He could milk, ride a horse, or act as a tarboy in a shearing shed. When the drift to the towns began in the second half of the century the children of the lower orders were soon at work. The worst that was said of some of them was that they absorbed something of the ruthless attitude of the previous generation; they were seen to practice flogging and had been known to strike servants with their whips. Significantly, they considered themselves as 'inheriting a *right* in the land of their birth, which no foreigner can alienate or possess'.

Even by 1806 their gambling habits were notorious, and youngsters were to be seen on the Sabbath playing 'chuck farthing'; later they were accused of playing too much at cards. Dr. James Kilgour described their activities: 'The relaxation enjoyed by manhood and youth is not usually of that laborious description which constitutes the amusement of the village green in the old country; putting the stone, throwing the hammer, and such like sports appear less congenial to the disposition of the idler than the gentler exercise of quoits or bowls, which afford suitable excitement without fatigue, and are better adapted to the slighter muscular system of the Australian youth' — but he was writing of Victoria. Laziness or idling, the preference for a chat rather than work, or a glass of grog in a public house to a cup of tea at home, are comments which appear as the nineteenth century progresses.

By the middle of the century a note of usually tolerant criticism is often to be found. Frank Fowler in 1859 was 'much delighted ... with the colonial young stock. The Australian boy is a slim, hard-eyed, olive-complexioned young rascal fond of ... cricket and chuckpenny, and systematically insolent to all servant girls, policemen and new-chums. His hair is shiny with grease, as are the knees of his breeches and the elbows of his jacket. He wears a cabbage-tree hat, with a dissipated wisp of black ribbon dangling behind, and loves to walk meditatively with his hands in his pockets, and if cigarless, to chew a bit of straw in the extreme corner of his mouth'. He could fight but 'otherwise he is orientally indolent'.

'Lazy as he is though, he is out in the world at ten years of age, earning good wages, and is a perfect little man, learned in all the ways and by-ways of life at twelve or thirteen ... for shrewdness, effrontery and mannish affectation, your London gamin pales into utter respectability before the young Australian.' He never spoke 'without apostrophising his "oath"', and interlarded 'his diction with the crimsonest of adjectives. . . . The prattle of the little urchins in the street bristles all over with objurations and anathemas'. The same observer observed that 'like the boys, the young ladies of Australia are in many respects remarkable. At thirteen years of age they have more ribbons, jewels, and lovers, than perhaps any other young ladies of the same age in the universe. They prattle — and very insipidly too — from morning to night. . . . Generally, the colonial damsels are frivolous, talkative and overdressed'.

Another observer, in 1893, considered that too often the Australian native youths had 'the self-sufficiency that is begotten on self-confidence by ignorance'. 'Lean and high-strung, with the alternations of languor and activity which the terrible changefulness of their climate gives them, they wear themselves out in all they do, mistaking the exercise of nervous energy for pleasure'. However, they were 'wonderfully free from cant, and when not suspicious of patronage or irony ... endowed with much simple friendliness'. The girls were restless, frank and energetic, with 'little prudery, and ... well able to look after themselves'.

George Walters in the *Sydney Quarterly Magazine* (1889) looked down on the young Australians in very much the Victorian manner — the young Australians 'who cannot fully sympathise with the home feeling of their parents, and who look upon the welfare of the colony as the supremely important question for them to consider'. Too many of the young men thought only of their daily work and popular sports, with too much of the great idol Mammon thrusting his presence into pleasure in the form of gambling. However, 'there is probably more of intellectual growth and more of earnest thought upon great questions among the young women. . .' who were taking an intelligent interest in the questions and problems of the day; 'they must be looked to for the salvation of the literary character of young Australia'. A growing national sentiment was present but was not sufficiently general, consisting far too much of 'a bitter and absurd prejudice against anything and everything British'. In fact, Australians were the inheritors of a long tradition, and if the young Australian could but rise 'to the importance and the sublimity of the occasion ... there is just the bare possibility that this great continent may become the home of a higher type of humanity'. This was to become a basic tenet of Australian nationalistic and socialist movements at the turn of the century.

Insofar as the family is concerned, it seems that the Victorian husband and father never quite achieved the same status in Australia as in England. The shortage of females gave them wide scope in their choice of a husband, and they did not entirely surrender their individuality, or their opportunity to escape with someone else, when they married. Certainly, father remained the head of the household, developing and preserving a sense of family stability and tradition. Morven Brown describes how, in the first decades of the century, it was the family activity which dominated the lives of the children — the family picnics, the annual family holiday, usually to the seaside, the elaborate family visits to relatives and the innumerable social activities at home. City life was still developing, and many of the entrants to the suburbs were newcomers, so that close 'village-type' relationships did not develop, and the solidarity of the family was enhanced.

Perhaps this solidarity led to insularity. R.H. Horne observed that 'the majority of the young men have neglected and lost their best opportunities of improvement, they possess no educational knowledge, no talents, accomplishments, or taste themselves, and they cordially hate and pretend to scorn and ridicule all those who possess any such acquirements'. Horne agreed with others in noting that they had 'no reverence, admiration or respect for any persons, talents or works of genius, and they substitute the arrogance of ignorant youth and the "game to fight" for all other qualifications'. In the background of a century of colonial development lies the origin of a cultural lack from which we have not escaped, and also the genesis of the contempt for the intellectual which still characterises the Australian outlook.

R.E.N. Twopeny gives a delightful account of the child in Australia. He admitted to a holy horror of babies 'but for general objectionableness I believe there are none to compare with the Australian baby.' This was only partly because the summer heat and sudden climatic changes made him worse behaved, but more because 'the little brute is omnipresent, and I might also add omnipotent'. The baby lived in the family circle almost from the time of its birth, for nurses and nurseries were rare. He was lashed into a chair by his mother's side at meals, he accompanied her on her household duties, and often when she was receiving her visitors. This might have been tolerable 'but the middle and lower classes of Australians are not content with the baby's supremacy in the household. Wherever his mother goes, baby is also taken. He fills railway carriages and omnibuses, obstructs the pavement in perambulators, and is suckled *coram populo* in the Exhibition. There is no getting away from him. . . . He squalls at concerts; you have to hold him while his mother gets out of the omnibus, and to kiss him if you are visiting her house'. Twopenny's attack continues 'It is little better when he gets old enough to walk and talk. Having once made the household bow down before him, he is slow to relinquish the reins of office. . . . If the child no longer cries or has to be kissed, he makes up for it in other ways. He has breathed the free air of Australian independence too early to have much regard for the fifth commandment. To make himself a nuisance till he gets what he wants is the art he first learns, and to this end he considers all means legitimate. . . . The child has no restrictions put on his superabundant animal spirits, and he runs wild in the most extraordinary, and often to elders, unpleasant freaks. When old enough to be distinguished by petticoats or breeches, the girls are a decided improvement on their brothers. Not that they have any great desire for intellectual improvement but she can at least strum the piano and above all she learns practical things such as how to cope with a household, and how to make herself a dress'. She was good humoured and fond of every kind of fun. Her home training led to little obedience or respect for her teachers and parental authority was constantly interposed to prevent well-deserved punishment. She began to attend grown-up dances at 13 or 14 but she cultivated a cameraderie with several men rather than hurried to catch a husband. She was jolly, with large hands and feet, no features and no figure, yet with 'a taking little face'. Brunettes by this time were in the majority. She was frank, full of good fellowship, and rarely affected. She had a keen perception of the value of money but did not take this into consideration in choosing her husband, who had to be a 'manly' type. Conversation with ladies and married people of either sex was scarcely worth her time but with a bachelor it was excellent. The Australian schoolboy had 'all the worst qualities of the English boy ... but few of his redeeming points. His impudence verges on impertinence, and his total want of respect for everybody and everything passes all European understanding. His father and mother he considered good sort of folk, whom he will not go out of his way to displease; his school master often becomes ... his worst enemy' with obedience but the last resort. He could ride as soon as he could walk and he was fond of all athletic sports, which unlike the English he persists with to young adult life. As he could easily pass his school days without having a single fight, 'he lacks the wholesome experience of a few good lickings', although he is quarrelsome and plucky enough. When at home for the holidays, his mother might try to dig some manners into him but he had 'far too great a sense of the superiority of the rising generation to pay more attention to her than is exacted by the fear of punishment'. Punishment was rare but lenient, 'public opinion being strongly against corporal punishment'. Indoors the Australian boy was more objectionable than the English because under less restraint. 'Generally intelligent and observant, he is here, there and everywhere; nothing escapes him, nothing is sacred to him.' Twopenny drew attention to the loss of distinction between the lower middle class and the upper middle class, a development which was excellent for the former but not so good for the latter. 'In the generation that is growing up, the levelling process is going much further. The small tradesmen's sons are going into professions and the professional men's sons into trades.'

At the beginning of the century the pattern of family life was advancing towards that of today. Both parents worked long hours, but with mother in the home and father largely out of it, the children recognised mother as the dominant influence in their supervision and in setting standards of behaviour, appearance and personal hygiene. Father was called on in major emergencies and to administer occasional severe penalties; corporal punishments, at least for boys, were a normal hazard of childhood well into this century. Not yet had the parents ceased to watch carefully and strictly over leisure activities but nevertheless the period saw the development of 'larrikinism' and the urban 'pushes'.

An anthropological view of the change at the turn of the century was offered by Dr. Alan Carroll: '... the Australians of all classes present a very favourable impression of their merits and behaviour.' He noted the development of a 'certain typical Australian form of head, face, body and limbs, in both the men and the women'. The men 'are as tall, strong and vigorous as the same classes of Britain and more so than any of the other Europeans we have seen and studied, and the women in masses brought together are as handsome and graceful as any large numbers of their sex we have noticed in Europe'. Australian crowds were not as emotional as European crowds and there was less drunkenness, horseplay or disorderliness than might occur in Europe. A further interesting development recorded by Carroll is that 'the large, tall, muscular, blonde people of the first and second generation are being superseded by the thinner, shorter, darker brunettes of the present,* so much so that it is only necessary to observe any three generations of most families and it will be seen how different are the first from the third generation'. Carroll considered the blondes as the more adventurous types of pioneers, whilst the brunettes became town dwellers, shrinking from rough work or new enterprise. It was also reassuring, as Pell showed in 1878, that the mortality rates for those aged about 50 years were lower in New South Wales than in England. As the Australian-born predominated in the relevant age groups, there was no evidence of physical degeneration attributable to the Australian climate or environment.

I concluded a detailed study of the heights of juvenile convicts and later Australian youths by noting that the first generation's 'striking and well-attested characteristics — its brashness, its independence, its self-reliance, its awkwardness and its capacity for heavy work at an early age — would all be enhanced or facilitated by an increase in height. As their fathers and mothers probably averaged only about 165 cm and 155 cm respectively, they may well have looked down upon the older generation, both literally and metaphorically, by the age of 15 or 16 years. Height, environment, intelligence, and perhaps also brain development, are intercorrelated phenomena. It is thus a reasonable hypothesis that the physical stature of the first generation both aided and reflected the attainment of a mental and moral stature which enabled them to turn away from the vices of their forebears, and to become "the theme of universal admiration"'. In the broader perspective of the present survey, it is impossible not to note the conflict between the observed end-result of a ghastly environmental and parental situation and the teaching of modern child psychology with its

* Harvey Sutton noted that blondes outnumbered brunettes by nearly 2 to 1 in Victorian schoolchildren c. 1915.

opposite emphases. The historical evidence indicates that hardship and struggle in childhood had a beneficial influence on character, no doubt at some cost in other ways.

References and further reading

Elkin, A.P. *ed. Marriage and the family in Australia.* Sydney, 1957 (especially chapters by W.D. Borrie and M.S. Brown).
Gandevia, B. *op. cit.* Chapter 6.
Hood, J. *Australia and the East,* etc. London, 1843.
Macnab, K. & Ward, R. The nature and nurture of the first generation of native-born Australians. *Historical Studies,* 1962, 10: 289.
Meredith, Mrs. Chas. *Notes and sketches of New South Wales, during a residence in that colony from 1839 to 1844.* London, 1861.
Twopeny, R.E. *Town life in Australia.* London, 1883.

9 EDUCATION, LITERATURE AND RECREATION

Train them and form them! Ah me! it is they who,
    unconscious, have wrought me
Back to the form that I bore when I bloomed as the
    darling of home.
I their preceptress! Ah me! with their innocent
    smiles they have taught me
Lessons more glorious than Greece, aspirations more
    lofty than Rome.

Brunton Stephens, *Convict Once*

Although these subjects cannot be overlooked because of their importance to child welfare, only a brief outline is offered here.

EDUCATION

Some school arrangements were made in the first years of settlement at Sydney, but the details are uncertain. Two convicts, William Richardson and his wife Isabella Rosson, were teaching school in Sydney in 1789. In 1791 the Reverend Johnson obtained the appointment of a First Fleet convict, McQueen, as schoolmaster on Norfolk Island, where King established a fund to support the school from an illegal duty on spirits. By 1796 Johnson himself was supervising schools, and by 1800 free schooling was available at Parramatta, Sydney and Kissing Point. In 1803 the *Sydney Gazette* advertised copperplate copy books and spelling books at the rather high price of sixpence, but for the most part textbooks were provided by such organisations as the Society for the Promotion of Christian Knowledge.

Governor Hunter encouraged the children by examining them himself and keeping samples of their written work for comparison with the following year. Although some of the children must have had paper and pens, the alphabet was usually taught on frames of moistened sand with a pointed peg; quills of the magpie and larger birds were used for pens when paper and homemade ink were available. The educational system became more firmly established under Governor Macquarie with an increase in the number of outlying schools to over 20. The chief, and recurring, difficulty of the early schools was to find competent and reliable teachers. Most came from the convicts, and occasionally, as at Moreton Bay, from the ranks of the New South Wales Corps. Sergeant Harry Parsons, bandmaster to the marines with the First Fleet, remained 'of very great Utility to the Colony as Instructor of Sacred Music to the little female orphans' until his death in 1819, perhaps an outstanding example of the voluntary aid which must have been widely given. Sunday schools, of special importance when children earned a living during the week, were formally instituted in Sydney in 1815.

In 1825 Archdeacon T.H. Scott returned to Australia with, in effect, a commission from the Secretary of State to establish a comprehensive educational system ranging from infant schools to tertiary institutions. This was to be administered under a Church and Schools Corporation largely controlled by the Church of England. With some financial backing from the local government, the number of schools in New South Wales under its jurisdiction increased from 16, with 1,037 children, to 36, with 1,855 children, in 1829, and to 40 (2,426 children) in 1831. The orphan schools became better supervised, so that there was no longer a 'loathesome and horrid state of disease and filth' to be found amongst the children. This Anglican, or establishment, control of the educational system could not continue indefinitely; towards the middle of the century in New South Wales there was a state school system and a state-aided denominational system. Victoria introduced the first comprehensive system of free, secular and compulsory education in 1872, while in New South Wales state aid was abolished in favour of a state system in 1880. By 1900 education was firmly established on a non-sectarian basis in all states, and in the next decade or so governments also entered the field of secondary education with the development of technical and high schools. Parallel with these changes, the Roman Catholic Church gradually evolved its own system, building on foundations established during the period of state aid.

The first attempts to establish private or grammar schools began in Sydney in Governor Hunter's time, the primary aim being to provide an alternative to sending the children of the more successful colonial families to England. There were many ephemeral private schools or academies, but the leading boys 'public' schools, often established with government subsidy in some form, received encouragement and stimulus from the establishment of universities in Sydney (1850) and Melbourne (1853), which set matriculation standards. The concern of the Reverend Marsden's wife at parting with her very young children has been mentioned, but perhaps a more common family pattern is indicated in the reminiscences of George Suttor. A humble but successful settler, of moderate education himself, he expressed his regret at 'the want of good schools and education for our numerous and industrious family'. The boys were 'obliged to tend the ewes and cows' in the early days, especially when the maintenance of assigned servants became expensive But his youngest son was able to attend the King's School at Parramatta and then complete his tertiary education in England. Similar educational institutions for girls were slower to evolve; although Lady Jane Franklin made detailed plans for an elitist school for Hobart's young ladies in the late 1830s, most private schools for girls did not emerge until late in the nineteenth century. Despite all the difficulties of education, Goodin concludes that the Australian-born children were more literate than their parents as judged by ability to sign the marriage registers between 1804 and 1814.

Distance and transport have necessarily influenced Australian educational practice. The origin of correspondence schools dates back to 1914. Use was quickly made of radio, including the famous 'pedal wireless', originally introduced in conjunction with the Flying Doctor Service; the Queensland School of the Air was a pioneering venture. One of Australia's first educational works (1848) was aimed at mothers who were obliged to teach their own children. In view of the 'tyranny of distance', it is perhaps remarkable that the administration of education remained firmly centralised in the capital cities, with little local participation or contribution. On the other hand, as Jungfer points out in relation to South Australia, after the introduction of compulsory education the primary school and its teacher often played a central role in the community in rural areas. Henry Lawson saw differences in town and country educational facilities:

> It was built of bark and poles, and the roof was full of holes
>   And each leak in rainy weather made a pool...
> And we learnt the world in scraps from some ancient dingy maps
>   Long discarded by the public-schools in town;
> And as nearly every book dated back to Captain Cook
>   Our geography was somewhat upside-down.

Pre-school education was carried out largely on a voluntary or private basis until well into the twentieth century. Kindergarten movements began in New South Wales in 1895, Victoria in 1901, South Australia in 1905 and in other states between 1906 and 1912. More than 20 years elapsed before the Lady Gowrie pre-school centres were established in the capital cities as a result of Vera Scantlebury Brown's initiative and the support of the Federal Ministry of Health. By this time Froebel's original concept of the kindergarden as a place where games and play were educationally orientated was a century old. The Australian Association for Pre-School Child Development was formed in 1938.

At the turn of the century, the medical profession, as an extension of its concern with infant welfare, was also interesting itself in the schools, partly as potential centres of education in hygiene, partly as the unhealthy sources of spinal curvature and other deformities, and partly as areas offering fertile scope for preventive medicine, early diagnosis and correction. One of the first school surveys, in Queensland in 1907, revealed many cases of visual defect, and in 1908 J.S.C. Elkington, chief health officer in Tasmania, produced an excellent book on *Health in the School or Hygiene for Teachers,* in an attempt to help and encourage teachers to meet their new responsibilities in these fields. School medical services were initiated in Victoria in 1909 and in South Australia in 1913; both were concerned to teach teachers, as well as inspect children. J.W. Springthorpe, in his textbook of therapeutics, dietetics and hygiene (Melbourne, 1914) gives a comprehensive review of the medical aspects of schooling. He attributed a decline in the physique and health of the current generation to 'teacherdom which neglected the bodies, which never qualified itself to impart the knowledge of protection from health and disease ... the same teacherdom is with us now, resisting the medical inspection of school children ... prattling of child-soul gardens, and manufacturing child-body cess-pools; spending years in teaching how to model baby-elephants in plasticene, and never an hour on how to use a tooth-brush; dawdling over book-learnt nature study, in dark, over-crowded class-rooms, redolent with the air-sewage of unwashed children'. He advocated physical education (a suggestion first put forward in the 1880s), the creation of open-air schools, medical and dental inspection, school nurses, and the need to teach girls a measure of science and domestic economy to ensure that they could bring up children with due attention to hygiene and health. He laid down guidelines for the design of schools but did not ignore the need to develop proper moral and religious attitudes, and the proper use of leisure. Springthorpe's holistic approach to schooling reflected medical recognition at this period of a close relationship between environment, health and disease (both mental and physical), and a rapidly growing interest in preventive medicine as a major part of public health. In part, the inspiration came from the belief that Australia offered the opportunity for the development of a new 'super-race', an idea akin to socialist philosophy, widely manifest at the same period, which idealistically saw Australia as the Utopia of the common man. Be that as it may, medical influence towards change in educational practice contributed to enhanced public awareness of hygiene, and thus almost certainly made a contribution towards the steady decline in child mortality discussed in later chapters.

Schools have never lacked critics. The newly established infant school at Parramatta received its share from a journalist in 1828: in singing and recitation 'we would recommend a *lower* key, for really the sounds of their uplifted voices have not yet ceased to ring upon our ears'.

LITERATURE

Children's literature in Australia developed slowly, but perhaps took no longer for its local character to evolve than adult prose and poetry. The first children's book to be written and published in Australia appeared in 1841; it contained 'tales of shipwrecks and aborigines' but most of the stories to emerge in the next three decades were of a highly moralistic tone. Adventure stories for boys, as well as Australian fairy tales, embodying the local flora and fauna, began to appear about 1870. Ethel Turner's long series of novels commenced with *Seven Little Australians* in 1894. Mary Grant Bruce's 'Billabong' series started in 1910, shortly after Mrs.

Aeneas Gunn's factual *A Little Black Princess* (1904). For younger readers the peak of the fairy tale was reached with May Gibbs' *Snugglepot and Cuddlepie* (1919), its value much enhanced by the authoress' delightful illustrations. By this time Australian children's literature covered a wide range of subjects in competent fashion, and even authors of works for adults, such as Norman Lindsay, Charles Barrett and E.J. Brady, occasionally wrote for children. Adult authors were not unaware of childhood problems, and many of the quotations in this book are chosen to illustrate this point. In less serious vein, there were innumerable editions of *Cole's Funny Picture Books* from 1876, very much period-piece collections of verse and illustrations, the latter often of a surprisingly high standard.

No doubt partly as a response to a growing literacy as much as to the developing literature, special children's libraries, or sections of larger libraries, were established in the second decade of the twentieth century. A juvenile section was opened at the Sydney Municipal Library in 1912, in Adelaide in 1914 and in Prahran, Victoria in 1918. The first lending library for children was also created in the Sydney Municipal Library in 1919. A year later the Public Library of New South Wales began to provide a special library for rural schools; services of this kind are now widespread.

It is difficult to estimate, or perhaps overestimate, the long-term benefits to child welfare of the universal ability to read, or to assess the impact of this new literacy on the social developments of the twentieth century. Ability to read enabled the production of technically competent books and pamphlets on health, hygiene and nutrition, aimed particularly at the young housewife and mother, and through her, at her children. Many of these were freely contributed by doctors, for example, to the Australian Health Society, with no thought of profit, and similar publications were produced or subsidised by governments, especially after 1920. For schools, hygiene and biology posters were distributed by similar voluntary agencies. Today, television poses a threat to reading, and shows little sign of developing its educational potential; its influence, for better or for worse, is a controversial issue.

RECREATION

Apart from the gambling activities noted earlier, and the more genteel game of snap-dragon at Government House, there is little information on the recreation of the children of the early settlements; no doubt they made their own amusements, perhaps with the encouragement of the old sailor or soldier who appears so often in English children's novels of the period. A pattern does begin to emerge by the middle of the century, when cricket and rowing established themselves as the popular 'team' sports; Sydney College played cricket on Hyde Park in the 1830s. Athletics, including walking races, were also part of the weekend amusements of the people; walking and running races were commonplace, and the primary school sports day in rural areas was an important community event by the 1860s. Australian Rules football owes its origins in about 1858 partly to the interest of private schools in Victoria; sportsmen were looking for a winter game perhaps more appropriate to the local climate and hard ground than the evolving English game of rugby. Footballs and cricket bats were issued to Victorian industrial schools. For those fortunate enough to have access to a court, tennis became an appropriate game for both sexes to enjoy late in the nineteenth century.

Boating outings and picnics at the seaside must have enlivened many a childish day over many decades but swimming was not a widely accepted form of recreation before the 1900s. Possibly life was less inhibited for country youngsters: Henry Lawson recalled the days 'we played the wag from school' and 'the times we went in swimming' (naked, incidentally). The increasing interest in swimming led to the surf lifesaving movement after the first world war.

The development of sporting activities was facilitated by the progress of the 'eight hours day' movement from the 1860s and the gradual general acceptance of Saturday afternoon as a half-holiday. Thus, it was more than the climate which enabled boys of the Victorian era to excel 'in out-door exercises' and to develop 'muscular Christianity'.

References and further reading

Goodin, V.W.E. Public education in New South Wales before 1848. *Journal of the Royal Australian Historical Society,* 1950, 36: 1, 65, 129, 177.
Saxby, H. *A history of Australian children's literature 1841-1941.* Sydney, 1969.

10 THE ERA OF INFECTIOUS DISEASES

Will you not wait for the children, Time,
And hurry us home instead?
Ah, Time, wait for the children!

W. Ogilvie, *Time and the Children*, 1913

INTRODUCTION

The commencement of this period *circa* 1850 is characterised by increasing autonomy and independence of the several colonies which had also shared in varying degree the maturing experience of weathering a recent economic recession. Although copper mining had begun in South Australia, and gold was soon discovered in New South Wales, these events were rapidly overwhelmed by the rush to the Victorian fields. This siphoned off population from other states, especially Tasmania, and attracted large numbers from overseas. In many ways, then, the first decade of the period was one of change. It is simpler to take up the story again around 1860, when the demographic situation is beginning to stabilise, and relatively reliable census returns and vital statistics are becoming available. In discussing this period I shall draw chiefly on data for New South Wales, with only brief reference to the other colonies where this seems appropriate.

By 1861 the population of New South Wales was approximately 350,000, two-thirds of them in the country. The masculinity ratio, although it had worsened a little with the gold migration, was 1.3, a vast improvement on 40 years previously when there were about 3 males for each female; among urban young adults the distribution of the sexes was even. As an illustration of the similar patterns of evolution in the several states, although at different times, the masculinity ratio was 1.3 in Western Australia in about 1881 but had increased to 2.1 a decade later in response to its gold rush. In 1861 in New South Wales 38% of the population was under 15 years of age, and 16% was aged less than 5 years; only 1.3% of the population was aged over 65 years. In Sydney almost half the population was under 12 years. The community contained some

50,000 married couples. The people lived in 57,400 houses of all kinds containing 230,000 rooms; two-thirds of the homes were 'weatherboard, slab and inferior'. Quaintly, there were in addition 7,000 tents and drays and 219 ships used as residences.

The birth rate was 341 per 1,000 married women under 45 years of age, by comparison with 302 in Victoria. In all states throughout the last half of the century there was a progressive decline in the birth rate, and by 1901 it was 235 in New South Wales and 229 in Victoria; in Queensland in the preceding two decades it had fallen from 316 to 254. This decline added impetus to moves to decrease infant mortality. The illegitimacy rate in New South Wales, expressed as the number of illegitimate births per 1,000 single women, increased only marginally from 15 to 16 between 1861 and 1901.

During this period several factors were operative to produce greater family stability than in the past. The demographic trends noted above in themselves operate in this direction. At the beginning of the period under review, a predominantly pastoral and agricultural economy and a predominantly rural population tended to keep families together as more or less independent and self-sufficient units, but the drift to the cities and the development of industries was already beginning to counter this influence. Even middle class families of moderate income had less in the way of servants than in Britain, chiefly because the quality of the servants remained as poor as in the convict era, and the Australian-born girls came to prefer ill-paid but independent factory work to this occupation. Hence even at this period wives were necessarily spending a good deal of time in home duties. At least in the bush, Australian men took a somewhat romantic view of women, but from marriage they expected something of the companionship which characterised their masculine 'mateship'. The wife largely gave up 'the pomp and vanities of which she had her fill during spinsterhood' and devoted herself to her household, children and husband, as one of several overseas observers of the Australian family commented. Her influence in the family circle became more firmly established as the father figure was never as dominant as in England and Europe at this period; in considering the first and later generations we have already seen that the children occupied a more prominent position than in families overseas, in part because of the lack of suitable people to employ as nursemaids. Even when the drift to the towns grew apace in the last quarter of the nineteenth century the harshest features of the industrial revolution in England were avoided. In general, the working-class family could aim at their own home in an Australian town or city, although inevitably there was a fringe group, of varying size according to economic circumstances, where even the weekly income of a child wage-earner was important to the family. Towards the end of the century there was widespread concern over women at work, partly because of concern that this would diminish their fertility or impair the health of their offspring. The problems of the underprivileged and underpaid workers and their families at the beginning of the move towards towns in 1860 is graphically recorded in a Select Committee report on the condition of the working classes in Sydney, which paints an appalling picture of juvenile delinquency and vagrancy, parental immorality and ignorance, squalid, overcrowded, insanitary living conditions, alcoholism and prostitution. The greatest difficulty and hardship would be the lot of the unmarried, widowed or deserted woman, and there were many of the latter after the wild days of the gold rush. In New South Wales and Victoria the place of the child in the labour force was reviewed. It was found in Sydney that the children in employment tended to be stunted physically and precocious mentally, as well as to suffer from premature decrepitude. Especially in certain industries there was exploitation by employers, both in terms of long working hours and low wages. The former, sometimes up to ten hours, tended to exclude youth from taking advantage of any educational opportunities, even at night. The wages, although low, did serve to stabilise the economy of a working-class family and keep it together as a viable unit; the elimination of child labour over the years could, and did, produce hardship. Late in the century, pre-employment medical certificates of age and health were required, but for these an inevitably inequitable fee was payable; doubt was cast on the value of this procedure when it was noted in Queensland that no child had failed the examination in a consecutive series of about 400. Children in industry were also exposed to serious moral risks, particularly where girls and boys were working together. In New South Wales, Select Committees of the Legislative Assembly produced much revealing information not only on the condition of the working classes of Sydney in 1860 but also on the employment of children in 1875-76 and again in 1912. Conditions of employment for children were gradually ameliorated, partly as a result of specific legislation, and partly as a result of legislation concerning compulsory education and the school leaving age. The attitudes of employers, parents and children to child labour changed independently of any legislation as socio-economic standards of the work force improved, and as better opportunities were seen to follow better education.

Medically, the period is of intriguing interest. It saw the widespread use of anaesthesia and Listerian methods in surgery, while in medicine the evolving clinical understanding of disease was associated with greatly improved methods of physical diagnosis, a better understanding of pathology and, with the development of the germ theory of disease, of causation. The end of the century increased the socio-economic problems of living for the working classes, but it brought a conceptually important therapeutic advance (antitoxin) and an invaluable diagnostic aid, the Röntgen ray, which set the stage for modern developments. Over the whole period the medical profession became increasingly involved in public health measures; in this country, more than in Britain, the doctors played a leading role in measures to improve all aspects of the environment, whether in relation to sanitation, atmospheric pollution by noxious trades and practices, or the household supply of water, food and milk. At the end of the century, the medical profession was also beginning to think in preventive terms, as it had already done in relation to infant mortality, and some doctors were calling for regular examinations of school children and, as a forerunner of many other occupationally orientated medical examinations, for sight-testing of railway and shipping employees.

It was also the period of conflict between the proponents of the miasmatic theory of disease and those who espoused the contagionist cause; the high incidence of the infectious diseases gave a note of urgency to the debate. The sanitary movement received considerable support from the miasmatic theory, and it is a paradox that a major public health movement should have been based on an incorrect doctrine. William Thomson, the leading advocate of the contagionist theory in Australia, used an epidemiological approach to demonstrate the transmission of disease by milk, fomites and, in the case of tuberculosis, hypothetical particles of dried sputum; he was by no means opposed to improvements in Melbourne's insanitary state (after all, much of its night soil was deposited in Fawkner Park, opposite his house) but in adopting these contagionist views he was accused of being so. In some ways, the argument was more relevant in Australia than in England, where progress in sanitary reform occurred before the contagionist doctrine gained momentum after the establishment of the germ theory.

In short, the whole pattern of modern medicine, including its concern with early detection of disease and preservation of health, was evolving with a rapidity greater than had been evinced at any time in the preceding millenium. Simultaneously, the whole complex pattern of modern society was also developing at a remarkable speed; changing attitudes to social responsibility, social philosophy, politics, government and religion, were manifest. In Australia, all men had the vote, there were secret ballots, and the land was there for the ordinary man to develop as his inheritance, or so it appeared to the idealists, if not to the squatters, who developed most of it. The trade union movement formally tried its strength, with less success than later, in the last decade of the nineteenth century, but labour, without significant organisation, and with little conflict, had made important gains in working hours and conditions of employment three and four decades earlier. Abuses of child and female labour were not among the initial interests of the labour movement, nor was health. There was a nationalist Australian journal, *The Bulletin,* and a rapidly expanding Australian literature in prose and poetry with a strongly nationalistic tone, sometimes naive, but compelling in its challenge. It is a fascinating period of change, much of which is mirrored in the evolution of childhood health and welfare; the Hospital for Sick Children, Melbourne, noted in its annual report for 1876 that 'the mortality of children in this colony is ... altogether the consequence of causes of a social nature'.

INFANT MORTALITY

With the establishment of the *Australian Medical Journal* in 1857 the medical profession quickly indicated its concern with childhood mortality. The reasons for this are not clear, beyond the stimulus of the availability of local statistics, in large measure based on the pioneer work of William Farr. There is some support for this suggestion, in that the Victorian and New South Wales Registrars-General both immediately drew attention to the relevant statistics. The New South Wales Registrar-General was concerned that mortality in London was approximately 22 per 1,000 people living and in Sydney 25 per 1,000, in spite of significant advantages in climate, situation and relative lack of overcrowding. He indicated that in London deaths under 2 years comprised 85% of deaths under 5 years (38% of total deaths), whereas in Sydney the comparable figure was over 90% (39% of total deaths). Because of differences in population structure, comparisons between these figures do not necessarily reflect so adversely on Sydney as he contended, but they do illustrate the magnitude of the problem. Beyond raising the question of contamination of the water supply by the lead pipes then in use, the Registrar-General carefully avoided discussing remedial measures or specific causes, confining himself to the generalisation that 'the great sacrifice of life ... exhibited ... is the result of a sinful degree of neglect and recklessness, which call for the most earnest consideration' by those entrusted with 'the education, the moral training, and the government of the people'.

In Melbourne it was argued on the basis of returns for one quarter of 1853, when many of the population were understandably 'living in a state highly incompatible with infantile life', that only 37% of the deaths occurred in children under 5 years of age but that 50% of these deaths occurred under 1 year of age. Again the figures effectively highlighted a problem whatever their true significance.

A major review by W.H. Archer is both more critical and more constructive. In the period 1854-57 the infant mortality was 20% of the births in Melbourne, compared with about 13% in the rest of Victoria. He quoted a variety of references, including district mortalities from Britain, to indicate that this childhood mortality was still favourable. The fallacy of calculating infant death rates in relation to total deaths was given as one of the reasons why infant mortality in the colony had been exaggerated. Archer went on to demonstrate the high summer mortality from diarrhoea and dysentery as a major cause of Victorian infant deaths; this contrasted with the situation in Great Britain where other infectious diseases, notably smallpox, were the chief causes.

To show the widespread nature of the professional concern and interest in infant mortality, the *Journal* was also one medium by which a controversy concerning morbidity and mortality in the orphan schools at Hobart was conducted (Chapter 3). Charles McCarthy trenchantly argued the excess of child mortality in Melbourne by contrast with rural areas, or London, and again demonstrated the excess mortality in the summer months. Drawing an ingenious distinction between causes of disease and of death, he instanced the meddling of ignorant women and the ignorance of clerics and others in advocating quack or homeopathic remedies as contributory to the latter. Mackenna, also of Melbourne, was perhaps the first to look critically at the nomenclature and certification of diseases, suggesting the inadequacy of 'teething' and 'debility', and a relationship of both to diarrhoea.

The *Sydney Magazine of Science and Art* attributed the infant mortality which disgraced its city to 'the absurd practice of feeding children on animal food which prevails', although it did not go so far as to subscribe to the assertions of a correspondent of the London *Times,* who wrote that 'the babies of Sydney were fed on a diet of beef steaks and brandy'.

In Sydney in 1867 Pell produced a careful analysis of mortality which showed that mortality under 1 year of age was 11% of live births, followed in successive years by mortality rates of 5% and 2%, falling to 1% at ages 4-5 years and 0.5% for those aged 5 to 9 years; mortality then remained at about 0.3% until early adult life. In England the respective figures were 15%, 6%, 4%, 2%, 2% and 0.6%. It was thus unequivocally established that, correctly expressed, the data showed a lesser mortality in New South Wales than overseas. Although he gave no figures, Pell stated that mortality was higher in metropolitan areas. At birth the expectation of life at the age of 1 year was 50 years in Australia, compared with 47 in England and 43 in Sweden. Apart from Archer's partial attempt, there seems to have been little contemporary examination of disease specific mortality.

Inevitably, W.F. Litchfield's review in 1909 gives a more comprehensive picture. Infant mortality for the period 1860-1873 for New South Wales as a whole varied between a minimum of 9% of births and a maximum of 12%, the mean being less than 11%. From 1874 to 1886 the mean was closer to 12% falling only slightly to about 11% up to 1903. At this time there was an impressive decrease to a rate of about 8% up to 1909. Sydney metropolitan mortality in the decade commencing 1880 was of the order of 17%, but in the following decade it declined to about 14% (there were fluctuations about these average levels). The metropolitan rate began to fall in advance of the state rate in 1899 and continued to decline thereafter, so that early in the twentieth century the two rates differed by only about 1%. Pell indicates that most of this difference was due to a reduction in deaths from diarrhoea. Over the period 1885-1897, sewage connection had been completed in the city and the supply both of water and of milk improved. No close statistical relationship between these events and the change in mortality could be demonstrated, and one is left more with an overall impression of correlated, but not necessarily causal, phenomena, with the implication that other factors were also operative.

Litchfield also showed that the infant mortality rates for all Australian states were less than 10% in 1908-9, except in Victoria, where they were marginally higher. All were below contemporary infant mortality rates for 17 other countries, including Britain, Scandinavia, various European countries and Chile. Birth rates, it may be noted, for all the Australian states lay between 25 and 30 per 1,000 of population. Incidentally, Breinl, reviewing Queensland vital statistics in 1921, demonstrated a relatively uniform decline in infant mortality in both northern and southern Queensland, taking this to indicate that tropical conditions alone were not necessarily a major factor in infant mortality; hot weather *per se* could not be implicated as a direct cause of infant mortality.

A.J. Turner, in 1910, wisely observed that the causes influencing infant mortality were not only medical but also social, economic and moral. On the latter aspect, he pointed to the rising percentage of illegitimacy in Queensland, a rise from 6% to 7.45% over a decade, whereas the rate in South Australia was only 4.4%. He gave a pertinent breakdown of the deaths in Queensland for 1908. The first group comprised approximately a third of the deaths under 1 year, and consisted chiefly of congenital disorders, including syphilis, about which little could be done. A second group comprised diseases which were reasonably well understood, or at least appreciated, namely infections of various kinds, comprising approximately 20%. The remainder were deaths due to diarrhoea and gastrointestinal disorders, the majority occurring during the summer months.

The later decades of the nineteenth century were a period of growing literacy amongst the population and of increased public education in hygiene. Books were published on the subject with increasing frequency by the turn of the century, one of the prototypes being J.G. Beaney's *Children: Their Treatment in Health and Disease* published in Melbourne in 1873. Dr. L.L. Smith was publishing numerous 'medical household sketches' in a non-medical journal (including one on why mothers did not suckle their own children) at the same period, and his *Medical Almanac* with its special appeal to young mothers, had been appearing since 1865. In Melbourne from 1876 the Australian Health Society, with professional support, published pamphlets on such matters as 'What kills our babies' containing practical and sensible advice, not necessarily always scientifically sound in retrospect, but nevertheless appropriate; there was a less active counterpart in Sydney.

It will be profitable to return to the question of infant mortality after considering the causes of disease and death in childhood. At this stage, it suffices to note that although the concern with infant mortality was partly based at the beginning of the period on misconceptions arising from the statistics, the medical profession showed a commendable persistence in attempting to study it and cope with it, even after the relatively sound position of this country was firmly established. Whilst it is true that publications in the local medical journals on the general subject of infant mortality declined after about 1865, they were replaced by papers on infant feeding and summer diarrhoea, which were in effect the only conditions which appeared preventable or treatable. Suggestions, not without foundation, are made by modern historians that interest in the health of child-bearing women over this period was influenced as much by socio-economic considerations as by humanitarian motives, but there can be no doubt of the dominance of the latter in the medical profession's interest in the survival of the children. It antedated concern about the physical development and health status of the working classes, it was independent of considerations of social class, and in no early contribution, even from statisticians, is there any suggestion of preserving or fostering a labour force.

CHILDHOOD MORTALITY

The pattern of disorders causing death is generally similar for all the colonies in the second half of the nineteenth century, although the infectious diseases showed fluctuations from year to year and from colony to colony according to the presence or absence of epidemics. Some of the causes then considered acceptable defy classification in modern times but they deserve note as reflecting the medical practice of the day. Chief amongst these was a group of disorders characterised by atrophy, debility, inanition or marasmus. Also prominent were convulsions, with which may be classified other 'neurological' disorders such as hydrocephalus, epilepsy and cephalitis. Teething, with which may be associated 'want of breast milk' and perhaps also gastritis, constitutes a third major group, while bronchitis and pneumonia were understandably common. Prematurity was also among the first ten causes of death, and there were the inevitable congenital malformations and inherited disorders, together with occasional causes of death such as scurvy, purpura, rheumatism and asthma. An indication of the frequency with which these contemporary diagnoses were certified as the cause of death is given below, but although the figures are based on published data they are not accurate for any place or period; they are intended only to give some idea of the relative importance of contemporary diagnoses in, say, a decade around 1875.

Atrophy, debility, marasmus, privation	15%
Diarrhoea and dysentery	15%
Brain diseases, epilepsy, convulsions cephalitis, hydrocephalus	13-26%
Bronchitis, pneumonia, lung congestion	7-13%
Teething, want of breast milk	5-10%
Prematurity	5-8%
Gastritis, stomach conditions	1-5%
Typhoid fever, enteritis	2-5%
Accidents	3%

The remaining deaths were contributed by the specific infections of childhood, and a variety of uncommon conditions.

The miasmatic, contagious or infectious diseases
In the early years of settlement the classical infectious diseases of childhood were absent. Their successive introduction often led to

explosive epidemics involving other age groups besides those of childhood, and often with a high case fatality rate. As the population grew these diseases tended to become endemic, with epidemic phases in which the more conventional age distribution of cases was found, usually with a somewhat lower mortality than previously but individual epidemics and diseases varied. The following summaries are based largely on the detailed work of J.H.L. Cumpston, amplified by the later studies of H.O. Lancaster. The historical epidemiology of these disorders in a country as isolated as Australia contributes significantly to understanding of their behaviour, as Australian experience, although perhaps not unique, was well documented from about 1855.

Owing to the lack of definitive diagnostic criteria and a multiplicity of synonyms for leading features, there are problems of interpretation of the data available in statistical returns. This problem arises with diphtheria, with typhoid and typhus fevers and the gastrointestinal disorders generally, and to a lesser extent in tuberculous diseases. In dealing with the epidemiology of all these disorders in the several colonies in summary fashion it is not possible to examine these questions in detail; the interested reader is referred to the critical assessments in the works of Cumpston and Lancaster. It is feasible only to make superficial use of the statistical data as a means of comparison and to indicate orders of magnitude; although I have frequently made detailed calculations I have often summarised them in generalisations which, whilst I trust not inaccurate, are necessarily approximations.

Whooping cough. Whooping cough appears to have been the most effective of the infectious diseases of childhood in surviving the long sea voyage; in 1828 it was the first epidemic disease to appear in Sydney (other than influenza and mumps), whilst it first occurred in Western Australia and probably Tasmania in 1833. By the middle of the century it was known in all states. The disease seems readily to have adapted itself to a colonial existence, and epidemics occurred every two to four years. Mortality in these years tended to be around 40 per 100,000 of population prior to 1880, falling to 30 prior to 1900 and then to 20; in inter-epidemic periods the mortality was often below 1 per 100,000. Over 95% of the deaths were under the age of 5 years. To judge by notification rates in South Australia, the case fatality rate was commonly between 1 and 3%, occasionally 6%, and in 1909 it was 21%. Victorian figures suggest that 46% of city children at the age of 5 years had had whooping cough, rising to 58% at the age of 9 years and 63% at the age of 15. Amongst country children only about one-third had had whooping cough by the age of 5 years and two-thirds by the age of 10, with a peak of 83% at the age of 14.

Measles. Measles was thought to have first appeared in Australia in 1850, but from a review of the deaths by age group in subsequent epidemics, Donovan postulated the existence of an epidemic in the mid-1830s, and further investigation revealed unequivocal evidence of an epidemic at this time which spread from Sydney to Tasmania and thence to New Zealand. The disease was reintroduced to Melbourne in 1850 and appears to have remained present until the explosive increase in population in the gold rush of 1853 produced a large epidemic with a high mortality of 55-60 per 100,000 of population in 1853-54. Thereafter there were epidemic waves at intervals of five to six years, occurring more or less simultaneously in all states, with the exception of Western Australia, where the disease appears to have died out between 1860 and 1883. There is usually some correlation between epidemics in Britain and Australia, suggesting that reintroduction may have played a part, but the disease was undoubtedly endemic in the larger states. After 1900, epidemics more closely followed the pattern of nineteenth-century Britain in that there was a two-to-three-year periodicity but also a dramatic fall in the mortality rate, even in epidemic years. The disease became notifiable in South Australia in 1909, and the figures indicate that even in this year of moderately high mortality the case fatality rate was less than 1%. The morbidity rate for clinical disease was 12 per 1,000 in this year, but in 1925 this reached 27 per 1,000. As a rule, about three-quarters of the mortality occurred before the age of 5 years, by which age (at least in the twentieth century) nearly 70% of children had had the disease. This figure rose to nearly 90% by the age of 10.

Diphtheria. There are particular diagnostic problems in relation to diphtheria and to some extent to scarlet fever; both might be described as 'cynanche' or 'angina' or simply sore throat, perhaps qualified as malignant. There is also the particular difficulty of 'croup' and of 'laryngitis'. Cumpston reasonably groups diphtheria and croup together, and points out that the statistical returns differentiate the epidemiological behaviour of scarlet fever and diphtheria, whatever minor accuracies there may have been. Croup was present in Australia before the specific diagnosis of diphtheria was first made in 1858, and is well documented in Melbourne and Sydney as a cause of death from time to time. The absence of a false membrane was regarded as the rule, so that the diagnosis of croup prior to 1858 probably implied a non-diphtheritic origin in most cases.

The behaviour of diphtheria differed in the several states, and also from European experience, making a summary difficult in all but very general terms. It appeared first in Victoria in 1858 (possibly with isolated cases in 1857). The first fatal case occurred in October, when the first known tracheotomy in Australia was performed by James Rudall on the third case of diphtheria, unfortunately with a fatal outcome. At about the same time the disease appeared in South Australia and Tasmania. There is no evidence as to its source, but its appearance coincides with a severe exacerbation of the disease in Britain. In Queensland and Western Australia the disease did not appear until the 1860s, while in New South Wales and

Tasmania its appearance was apparently not associated with a dramatic epidemic, such as occurred in Victoria and South Australia — perhaps coincidentally, these were the colonies in which the most striking population increases were occurring. In these two states the mortality rate rapidly reached approximately 150 per 100,000 of population, and a similar level was attained in Western Australia a few years later. Once introduced, the disease became endemic, with periodic epidemics in all states showing a general tendency towards a decline in mortality rates, both in epidemic and inter-epidemic periods. Paradoxically, in Tasmania the death rate rose from relatively low initial levels to a maintained high level between 1870 and 1880. In Western Australia mortality rose sharply in the early 1880s, and there was a sharp rise in Victoria between 1888 and 1890. Despite the fluctuations in mortality, which reflected epidemic morbidity, there is little clear evidence of periodicity and little correlation of the peaks amongst the several states.

In all states the mortality from diphtheria declined between 1892 and 1895, in which year diphtheria antitoxin was introduced. For the next 15 years (except for an epidemic period in Western Australia, *circa* 1908) mortality rates in all states remained remarkably constant, and although there is no further decline after the introduction of antitoxin, there does appear to be an 'ironing-out' of the previous fluctuations. In spite of increasing use of antitoxin, there is a general trend towards an increase in mortality after 1910, although not to the relatively high levels even of inter-epidemic periods obtaining prior to 1880. By 1900 mortality rates had fallen below those of England and remained so.

Some of the variability in death rates may be attributed to two factors: first, the tendency for the disease particularly to attack the 5 to 15 years age group but to produce the highest case fatality rates in the under 5 years age group, and second, the changing age distribution of the population. In Victoria, for example, the proportion under 5 years fell from 17% in 1861 to 10% in 1921, whilst there was little change in the proportion in the 5 to 15 years age group, namely about 20%. This in itself would account for some decline in the mortality rate. Cumpston also demonstrates a relationship of mortality to birth rate, that is, to the supply of susceptible individuals. Further, if the transmissibility of the disease is accepted as somewhat less effective than that, for example, of measles, the more gradual impact of the disease on the less densely populated states of Tasmania and Western Australia may be partly explained. In spite of these arguments, variations in the virulence of the organism appear to be major considerations; the later recognition of three strains of the diphtheria bacillus of different pathogenicity may explain some of the epidemiological peculiarities of the nineteenth century.

To give an indication of the deaths caused by diphtheria, the mortality rates per 100,000 of population were about 100 or more in the first decade of the disease in Victoria and South Australia, with a minimum of about 28 prior to 1890. Levels below 10 became common in most states in the first decade of the twentieth century but tended to rise to a maximum of 28 in the following decade. Morbidity rates tended to be high at the turn of the century, to decline in the first decade, and then to rise to maxima of 400 or 500 per 100,000 of population. Over the same period, case fatality rates declined from about 20% to between 2 and 5%. From the 1860s to the beginning of the third decade of the twentieth century the age distribution of deaths tended to change; the figures differ in the several states but, as an approximation, the proportion of deaths aged under 5 years fell from 75% to 50%, whilst at the other extreme, deaths over the age of 20 increased from about 1% to 4% of the total. To put the disease in due paediatric perspective, it may be noted that 10% of all notifications and 4% of deaths in New South Wales *circa* 1920 were in adults. Between 2 and 5% of notified cases were aged under 1 year, about 36% up to 5 years and 40% between 5 and 15 years.

The introduction of the Schick test (described in 1913) permitted a view of the obverse of clinical diphtheria, namely susceptibility. Figures from Melbourne in 1925 indicated that 100% of subjects aged 2 years were susceptible, 81% at 3 years and 60% at 5 years. Between 10 and 13 years the Schick positive rate was only 30%, and it is an interesting reflection of the previous epidemiology of the disease that over 50% of those aged more than 14 years were immune. The use of the Schick test paved the way for effective mass immunization, which became feasible at about the same time. Harvey Sutton estimated that by 1934 about 80% of Sydney's school leavers were immune. Incidentally, it was a matter of comment that country children and children of more affluent parents showed lower immunity rates because of their relative isolation.

An interesting feature in the history of diphtheria was the controversy over the role of tracheotomy, and, after 1891, of intubation, which was less traumatic and probably less hazardous at that period. A rational appreciation of the roles of these methods became possible only in the late 1890s with the clear differentiation between toxaemic and suffocative deaths which the concept of a specific toxin made possible. Diphtheria was one of the first diseases for which effective surgical and medical treatment became available, and their integration was not immediately apparent. Public awareness, or acceptance, of emergency tracheotomy is reflected in C.H. Souter's poem, *A Tight Corner:* 'Look, man, look at her lips! Don't you see they're quite blue?'

Scarlet fever. Scarlet fever probably first occurred in 1833, in Tasmania, the year in which puerperal fever is also first recorded, but the earliest epidemics were in Victoria and New South Wales in 1841. In other states it became significant in the 1850s but no case is recorded in Western Australia before 1865. From 1860 scarlet fever was endemic in all states except Western Australia, as it probably had been for more than a decade in the more populous states.

Whatever uncertainties there may be about the severity and magnitude of earlier epidemics of scarlet fever, there is no doubt of severe epidemics in Victoria and Tasmania in 1853, with a relatively high mortality, and an even more severe epidemic in South Australia in 1863-64. Records suggesting an epidemic in Sydney between 1858 and 1860 may in part represent the pandemic of diphtheria; the latter term appears to have been adopted later in Sydney than in Victoria. All states except Western Australia shared the most severe epidemic of all in 1875-77, with high mortality rates which were never again approached. Throughout the rest of the nineteenth century and the first decades of the twentieth there were numerous epidemics in all states, reflected in the latter part of the period in notification rates, which show no clear correlation between states. Nonetheless, despite some fluctuations, the mortality rate remained low. The epidemics also show little relationship to major epidemics in Britain. Scarlet fever was a disease widely accepted as miasmatic in origin, and hence it figures prominently in the sanitary and popular literature, although through most of its existence it was not in fact a disease greatly to be feared by comparison with some of the other infectious diseases of childhood.

Cumpston's data permitted a similar conclusion for scarlet fever as for diphtheria, namely, that the disease attacked particularly the 5-15 years age group but was more often fatal in the 0-5 age group, a generalisation applicable more especially to the years before 1880. Changes in the age constitution of the population cannot explain the dramatic changes in mortality, and there is no correlation between the death rate from scarlet fever and the birth rate.

Figures relating to Victoria may be taken to illustrate the foregoing generalisations. The mortality rate in 1853 reached 66 per 100,000 of population and then declined to 2 before rising again to 161 in 1861. There were irregular fluctuations in mortality until the remarkable peak of 280 per 100,000 in 1876, an epidemic in which nephritis was a common complication. This fell rapidly to 10 in 1882, a figure never again to be reached; from 1885 the mortality rate was only occasionally above 2, somewhat lower than in Britain. Case fatality rates were usually below 2% from 1898, although morbidity rates rose above 200 per 1,000 on several occasions up to 1925. Whereas two-thirds of the deaths occurred in children under 5 in the 1860s, this had fallen to 48% by the 1920s, but the overall number of deaths is small in later decades. The age distribution of notifications in New South Wales 1913-1924 was 2% under 1 year, 18% aged 1-4 years, 62% aged 5-14 years and 11% aged 15-24, reflecting a small trend towards more frequent infections in those less than 5 years of age at the expense of those aged 5-14 years. Over this period, the age distribution of deaths in New South Wales was approximately 5% under 1 year, 42% between 1 and 5 years, 33% aged 5 to 14 years and 10% aged 15 to 24 years.

Cumpston found no association in terms of annual mortality

between scarlet fever, erysipelas, puerperal fever, nephritis and pyaemia. There are many difficulties in establishing correlations of this kind, especially on the basis of relatively small numbers. While an association between scarlet fever deaths and deaths from nephritis might be expected, there was no excess of pneumonia or bronchopneumonia in the years in which measles was prevalent, presumably implying that the original disease was correctly certified as the cause of death. I am aware of no epidemiological data relating to rheumatic fever or rheumatic heart disease in this period, although 'rheumatism' was a common complaint by no means confined to the older age groups.

The Dick test for susceptibility was described in 1924; 70% of children were susceptible in their second year, falling gradually to about 18% at 20 years.

The enteric diseases. The important group of gastrointestinal disorders, notably dysentery and diarrhoea, is often inseparable in the records of the time from typhoid, typhus and even cholera. The position is further complicated by about 200 alternative names for these disorders. As they are primarily diseases of the total population rather than specifically of children, review of this subject must necessarily be brief; infantile gastroenteritis receives further attention in Chapter 14. Although cases of all these conditions appeared on ships from time to time, only dysentery and diarrhoea appear to have caused significant mortality in the colony itself prior to about 1850. Typhus was never of importance except in isolated and perhaps institutional epidemics, but typhoid was to become a major scourge as the size of cities and towns increased and hygienic conditions concomitantly deteriorated. Early in the third quarter of the nineteenth century the mortality from all these disorders must have increased, notably in relation to goldfield camps, but reliable data are lacking. In New South Wales, typhoid mortality was high, about 60 per 100,000 population from 1876 to 1878. After a respite when the mortality halved, it again rose to almost as high a level between 1882 and 1887. It then halved again for a decade but following a transient rise between 1895 and 1904 it fell progressively to less than 5 per 100,000 in 1920. The curves for typhoid and for all diarrhoeal diseases grouped together are roughly similar, with the mortality from all diarrhoeal diseases running at about 100 per 100,000 above that of typhoid until 1903, when the mortality from diarrhoeal diseases falls more steeply to be only about 40 above that of typhoid fever by the early 1920s. Diarrhoea and enteritis also show a similar pattern, but the mortality for these disorders under 2 years of age remained high, although fluctuating, around 100 deaths per 100,000 of population until 1904 when it fell to 60. Following a transient modest rise in the next decade it declined to a level of about 40 by 1920. Cumpston summarises a complex situation by stating that there was a uniformly high mortality from all these disorders prior to 1880, followed by a reduction first in dysentery, then in diarrhoea and enteritis over 2 years of age, then in typhoid fever and finally about 15 years later in the infantile diarrhoea and enteritis group.

Childhood deaths from typhoid fever were disproportionately high relative to total deaths prior to 1885. Thereafter the age distribution of deaths, with a peak proportion in the 15-30 years age group, remained unchanged until the 1920s, suggesting that progressive improvement in mortality was evenly distributed through all age groups; if an environmental factor were operative then it was operating equally throughout the population from 1885. Mortality rates for diarrhoeal diseases in the metropolitan area were approximately double those for the remainder of the state until 1890, when the city rates showed consistent and more rapid improvement, so that from 1900 the rates were the same. The pattern was somewhat similar for typhoid fever, except that after 1891 the rural rate (including mining areas) was higher than the metropolitan. In the first 20 years of the present century the notification rate for typhoid fever fell from about 25 per 100,000 of the population to less than 5 by 1920, with a consistently higher incidence in country areas.

The Victorian curves differ from New South Wales notably in very high death rates between 1854 and 1860 from dysentery and typhoid fever. South Australia is chiefly remarkable for a higher typhoid mortality throughout the whole period under review than New South Wales or Victoria; the mortality rate from this disease was still 20 per 100,000 in 1920. Taking all the diarrhoeal diseases together, the period of marked improvement was delayed until 1895. As in New South Wales, the deaths in each age group, expressed as a percentage of the total deaths, showed a gradual change such that mortality under the age of 5 years was uncommon after 1895. The outstanding characteristic of the typhoid mortality curve for Western Australia is the peak death rate of 350 per 100,000 coinciding with the gold discoveries of 1895-97, with a massive influx of migrants and comparatively little organisational control of hygiene. In Tasmania, it is interesting to note a phenomenon already mentioned in relation to New South Wales, namely, the more or less progressive decline in 'diarrhoea and enteritis' at all aged from 1880, while at the same time there is maintained a high mortality under 2 years of age from the same conditions. Although showing big fluctuations, there is little evidence of a decline in the latter curve before 1910.

Tuberculosis. Tuberculosis is also a disease of the general population but there are manifestations to which children were peculiarly prone. The disease was uncommon, certainly as a cause of death, prior to the middle of the nineteenth century in Australia. The influx of migrants at this period led to a high birth rate, and consequently in the following decades a high proportion of the population was both non-immune and in the more susceptible age groups. Numerous persons with tuberculosis migrated to Australia as a means of taking the cure, so that, together with those native-born who had acquired tuberculosis, there was an adequate pool of infection from which the rising generations could acquire the disease. Thus in all states, except perhaps Western Australia, there was a period of rising mortality from 1860 to about 1885, followed by a progressive decline, interrupted only by a small secondary rise in each state at some stage between 1900 and 1920, possibly related to the later phase of migration between 1880 and 1890 (a peak well seen in Western Australia). It is also likely that in the nineteenth century bovine infections were more significant, at least in non-respiratory tuberculosis.

In 1880-1882 mortality in the age group 0-4 years reached 260 per 100,000 of the population for males and 200 for females. Between the ages of 5 and 14 there was a dramatic drop to about 10 per 100,000, followed by a rapid return to high levels between the ages of 25 and 44 for males and 25 and 39 for females. By 1932-34, that is, after half a century without specific treatment or major systematic preventive measures, mortality in the 0-4 years age group for both sexes had fallen to about 12 per 100,000. Mortality was negligible during childhood until it began to rise at about age 15; for both sexes the now much reduced mortality was 60 per 100,000 at age 30 to 34. Mortality for women declined slightly at later ages, whereas for men it continued to rise to a peak in the 55-59 age group. J.W. Springthorpe's prediction in 1914 that tuberculosis mortality would be trivial in 25 years if current trends continued was fulfilled by contemporary, if not by modern, standards.

For non-respiratory tuberculosis, in 1910-12 the mortality rates of 0-4 years were approximately 40 per 100,000, dropping to 10 per 100,000 during the remainder of childhood. The female mortality rose earlier than the male, reaching 15 in the age group 15-19 years, whereas the male mortality approached this figure only in the 25-29 age group. There was little change in the mortality rates for non-respiratory tuberculosis with advancing age. By 1932-34, mortality in the 0-4 age group was about 13 per 100,000, declining during childhood to 3, and with both sexes thereafter showing a mortality of about 5.

It appears, both on epidemiological and bacteriological evidence, that bovine tuberculosis in childhood declined even more impressively than respiratory tuberculosis, which, as with bone and joint tuberculosis, was exclusively of human origin. Reginald Webster, the pioneer paediatric pathologist in Melbourne, isolated the bovine form of the bacillus chiefly from mesenteric and cervical glands and tonsils; in effect, it was more significant as a cause of morbidity than of mortality. Early in this century it was estimated that about 8% of Australian dairy cattle were infected but pasteurization had already been recommended, and extensive use of tuberculin testing in dairy herds was beginning. As an indication of the overall tuberculosis infection rate in adults, the von Pirquet test was positive in about 70% of adults, and about 20% of adults dying of any cause had demonstrably tuberculous lesions. The clinical diagnosis of respiratory tuberculosis at this period implied death within five years in about half of the cases. It is difficult to estimate the infant mortality of the nineteenth century attributable to tuberculosis; tuberculous meningitis and miliary tuberculosis were hidden in several of the descriptive terms mentioned earlier.

The striking feature of the epidemiology of tuberculosis is its rapid and virtually continuous decline long before the introduction of specific therapy. Early detection and sanatorium or 'isolation' measures reduced the risk of infection during most of the twentieth century, but cannot account for the overall decline of the disease, which began a decade or so earlier. Lancaster, using cohort analysis, has demonstrated the biostatistical influence of the change in age distribution of the population as it shifted towards the older age groups. Combined with public and professional appreciation of the mode of spread, the changing age constitution of the population offers a more effective explanation of the decline in the disease than the improving economic status of the community, despite an undisputed relationship of the latter to case fatality rate. To physicians in the nineteenth century tuberculosis raised many controversial issues, notably the relative importance of contagion and constitutional factors, the myth of the immunity of the Australian-born which had grown up in the first half of the century, and the illusion of a beneficial effect of the Australian climate. The susceptibility of the native-born, demonstrable by the 1870s, was a major factor in disposing of these misconceptions; the most effective epidemiological studies were those of William Thomson, whose outspoken views aroused most opposition.

It is of interest to note Koch's premature announcement concerning the prophylactic and therapeutic value of tuberculin in 1890, if only because of the enormous public interest generated by the news media of the day. After investigation of the situation, Professors Anderson Stuart (Sydney) and H.B. Allen (Melbourne) produced characteristically cautious and objective reports on its possible role. W. Camac Wilkinson, of Sydney and London, was to become one of the world's leading advocates of tuberculin therapy, but it was never evaluated adequately by modern standards. Its diagnostic and epidemiological value, first examined in Australia by J.W. Springthorpe, has been enhanced by the decline in tuberculosis, in contrast with the now almost forgotten skin tests formerly used to determine susceptibility to diseases such as diphtheria and scarlet fever.

Varicella and rubella. Although minor causes of mortality, it is appropriate to consider these briefly in relation to the other infectious diseases of childhood.

Chicken pox is perhaps the most likely of the infectious diseases to have gained early entry to Australia but its date of arrival seems to have passed unrecorded. References to it recur with every threat of a smallpox epidemic but although it assumed epidemic proportions from time to time — as, for example, in Victoria and South Australia in 1866 — it did not excite alarm. Perhaps the casual way in which it is mentioned does reflect early entry and endemicity. Varicella was suggested as a possible cause of the epidemic which decimated the Aboriginal population in 1789, but it is usually accepted that this was true smallpox, probably introduced from the north. The Aborigines suffered from 'native pox', a name probably including several disorders, one of which may have been varicella.

Rubella is of special interest because its unusual epidemiological behaviour permitted the detection of congenital malformations due to a maternal attack early in pregnancy. The earliest known epidemic was recorded in Victoria in 1867. The disease died out, for in 1873 during another epidemic attention was drawn to the surprising number of adults, especially women, who were attacked. A third epidemic, also in Victoria, occurred in 1883. There is no record of rubella in New South Wales prior to a major epidemic in 1898.

Deaf mutism was recognised by the statisticians, Knibbs (1917) and Wickens (1927) as showing epidemic fluctuations in incidence. Lancaster noted that no less than 70 of the admissions to the New South Wales Institution for the Deaf and Dumb were born in 1898, compared with an expected number of about 12, based on previous and subsequent experience. This was an epidemic year for rubella in Queensland, South Australia and Western Australia, but less evidently so in Victoria. Further review of admissions to the Victorian Deaf and Dumb Institute indicates that approximately double the expected number of patients were born in 1883-84, an earlier epidemic period.

Rubella is likely to have first reached Australia with the gold migrants in the early 1850s, a period immediately followed by a rising birth rate. It may be no more than coincidence that two deaf tutors should independently initiate classes for deaf children in Sydney and in Melbourne in 1860 (an appropriate latent interval), and that these efforts should rapidly receive public and government support. Formal institutions were functioning in both cities by 1861, and arrangements were soon made with Tasmanian and Queensland governments to support cases admitted from these states. The Victorian Institute for the Blind was founded in 1866, and in 1869 the Sydney institute extended its responsibilities into this area.

The contribution of rubella to stillbirths and to infant mortality is unknown.

SURVIVAL

The full impact of mortality on the family is difficult to appreciate from disease mortality rates or even infant mortality rates, and it may be made clearer by considering survival. In the 1880s, of every 100 children born, 90 at most might be expected to survive to the age of 1 year, 82 to 5 years and only 78 to adulthood. By the turn of the century, 90 might survive to 1 year, 88 to 5 years and 85 to adulthood. By about 1950, the respective figures were 97 and 96. Today, the parents of a child can expect it to grow up, whereas there was little more than a 3 in 4 chance of this in the middle decades of the nineteenth century. Indeed, increasing years of education for an increased proportion of children, the decline in child labour and the rising age of first employment mean that parents may now expect to look after and support their children well into adult life. More intimate glimpses of the effects of high child mortality in individual families are to be found not only in formal records but also in Australian prose and poetry; peculiarly tragic pictures are drawn in the popular health education and sanitary pamphlets of the late nineteenth century. Households might easily lose two or three children, and because of the age distribution of morbidity and mortality for some infectious diseases, the family in some cases might lose its mother or breadwinner, socially and economically an even more disastrous event than today. It is beyond our present scope to examine fluctuations in the birth rate, but a decline in birth rate was becoming a matter of considerable public and government concern by the turn of the century. The decline may be attributed largely to the introduction of more efficient methods of birth control and to wider usage amongst a more educated population. Indirectly, it gave impetus to measures aimed at preserving the lives of the infants who were born, while, contrariwise, parental realisation of the improved outlook for the survival of their children gave them some confidence in limiting their families. The circle may be completed by suggesting that fewer children meant more time for the mother to care for them effectively, and more money to feed them properly.

References and further reading

Archer, W.H. On the mortality of children in Victoria. *Australian Medical Journal,* 1859, 4: 139.

Cumpston, J.H.L. *The history of diphtheria, scarlet fever, measles and whooping cough in Australia, 1788-1925.* Canberra, 1927.

Cumpston, J.H.L. & McCallum, F. *The history of the intestinal infections (and typhus fever) in Australia, 1788-1923.* Melbourne, 1927.

Donovan, J.W. Measles in Australia and New Zealand, 1834-1835. *Medical Journal of Australia,* 1970, 1: 5.

Gandevia, B. William Thomson and the history of the contagionist doctrine in Melbourne. *Medical Journal of Australia,* 1953, 1: 398.

Lancaster, H.O. Tuberculosis mortality of childhood in Australia. *Medical Journal of Australia,* 1950, 1: 760.

Lancaster, H.O. Deafness as an epidemic disease in Australia: a note on census and institutional data. *British Medical Journal,* 1951, 2: 1429.

Lancaster, H.O. The mortality in Australia from measles, scarlatina and diphtheria. *Medical Journal of Australia,* 1952, 2: 272.

Lancaster, H.O. The mortality in Australia from typhus, typhoid fever and infections of the bowel. *Medical Journal of Australia,* 1953, 1: 576.

Lancaster, H.O. Infant mortality in Australia. *Medical Journal of Australia,* 1956, 2: 100.

Lancaster, H.O. The mortality of childhood in Australia. Part I, Early childhood. *Medical Journal of Australia,* 1956, 2: 889.

Lancaster, H.O. The mortality of childhood in Australia. Part II, The school ages. *Medical Journal of Australia,* 1957, 1: 415.

Lancaster, H.O. The mortality from violence in Australia. *Medical Journal of Australia,* 1964, 1: 388.

McDonald, D.I. Child and female labour in Sydney, 1876-1898. *Australian National University Historical Journal,* 1973-1974, nos. 10 & 11: 40.

11 MORBIDITY AND THE EMERGENCE OF PAEDIATRICS

Lord, whence sought we out the children that did languish?
When put forth the hand to make their burdens light?

Brunton Stephens, *For My Sake, c.* 1920

It is not surprising that some of the earliest medical literature published independently in Australia concerned paediatric subjects. The first separate publication of paediatric interest was Henry Jeanneret's pamphlet on the preservation of the teeth in 1830, followed by pamphlets on scarlet fever by William Bland (1841, and the first Australian contribution to clinical medicine) and Robert Little (1842). The first separate publication on a surgical subject, concerning strangulated congenital hernia, was by W.R. Pugh of Launceston (1845). Reviews of gastroenteric diseases and scarlet fever by T.F. Gorringe (Hobart 1850 and 1853) were followed by important contributions on these and the related problem of infant mortality by J.W. MacKenna (1858), C.E. Reeves (1867), both of Melbourne, and later by S.J. Magarey in Adelaide (1879-80), and John Service (Sydney, 1890). Perhaps one might have expected that the first medical libraries in Victoria and New South Wales would have included more than six or seven works of paediatric interest in their first 230 books.

Outstandingly popular, but professionally acceptable, books came from the prolific pen of Phillip Muskett between 1890 and 1910, dealing with all aspects of child care and childhood diseases. Part of the popularity of the numerous publications for lay readers was related to the isolation of many families, and 'every man his own doctor' was an unavoidable objective. Works by qualified practitioners such as *The Family Medical Index* by W.H. Jenkins (1874), George Fullerton's *Family Medical Guide* (six editions between 1870 and 1884), and T.P. Lucas' *Domestic Medicine* (1906, in a somewhat different style) were widely used and all contained a significant paediatric component. Beaney's contribution to infant management has already been mentioned; his works on spermatorrhoea (1870 and 1880) and on the generative system (1872-1883) contributed much alarming misinformation on the effects of masturbation; it was a widely held view that this practice led to insanity, imbecility and other disabling diseases.

The short-lived *Australian Medical Journal* (Sydney) for 1846 contains little of paediatric interest other than controversy over a case of infanticide and notes on some accidents to children. The main source of information from 1856 is Melbourne's *Australian Medical Journal* and its immediate successor, the *Intercolonial Medical Journal of Australasia,* which drew more interstate contributors. The *Australasian Medical Gazette,* published in Sydney from 1881, goes some way towards redressing a Victorian bias, but it was a decade or so before this journal achieved the same standard of original contributions.

The increasing interest in diseases of children is indicated by an average of eight items a year in the *Australian Medical Journal* in its first decade; the number doubled over the next two decades and doubled again in the last years of the century. There is an understandable concentration throughout the period on the infectious and diarrhoeal diseases and the associated phenomena of convulsions and teething.

In surgery, the most striking feature is the frequency of papers on the treatment of urinary calculi; there were no less than 17 references to this disorder and to lithotomy prior to 1876, after which either interest, or the problem, seems to have declined, although it drew papers in Sydney in the 1880s. The increasing scope of surgery is reflected in the attention given to intussusception, hernia and plastic surgery towards the end of the century, and contributions on hydatids were concerned partly with surgical aspects. Another feature is the developing interest in corrective orthopaedics, particularly for post-tuberculous curvature of the spine, and in the management of joint diseases (doubtless mostly tuberculous) and fractures, especially compound fractures. In the earlier decades, fractures of the skull were commonly reported, apparently in an effort to gain a better understanding of a confusing problem.

By the last decade of the century, specialisation was evolving, with many papers on ophthalmological and otorhinolaryngological topics. Deaths from chloroform, especially in the 1880s, were recorded in children, and also the use of local anaesthesia with cocaine. Another specialty to emerge in the later decades was dermatology.

Poisoning was a constantly recurring theme, and some of the causes reflect occupational, therapeutic and 'folk' practices of the day — aconite, opium or laudanum, Steadman's teething powders, carbolic and other acids, corrosive sublimate and creosote. Alkaloidal poisonings due to the consumption of plants or medicines were also frequent, and one indigenous cause was eucalyptus oil. As early as 1849 it had been pointed out to a Select Committee in New South Wales that, in relation to the unrestricted sale of poisons, 'the foolish and ignorant ought to be legislated for.' Snake bite was a common subject for discussion, particularly with the introduction of G.B. Halford's intravenous ammonia as a treatment, as well as Mueller's famous strychnine antidote. Halford's treatment, although unsuccessful and falsely conceived, did lead to practical experimental work, and it is also one of the earliest recorded uses of intravenous therapy.

In both Sydney and Melbourne journals, functional and hysterical disorders in childhood received their first mention towards the end of the century. There seemed to be an increasing interest in cardiac disease but few references to rheumatic fever, although passing references suggest that 'acute rheumatism' was not uncommon. Many medical conditions are discussed for the first time in individual articles, often reflecting rapid appreciation of advances overseas.

The geographical area from which the contributors were drawn is much enlarged by 1900, and a generally more scientific and less anecdotal approach is apparent. This is well exemplified by discussions on infant feeding, where consideration was given to the chemical composition of milk from different sources and of various artificial foods. The nutritional value of popular infant diets, often based on arrowroot and sago, was examined. Highly significant therapeutic advances recorded towards the end of the century were the introduction of tetanus and diphtheria antitoxins, important for their specific value but also because they reflected new scientific concepts and the possibility of developing new specific treatments.

It is worthwhile to review those names which recur sufficiently often in a paediatric context to indicate a special concern with the diseases of childhood. In the earlier decades, D.J. Thomas (surgery and infectious diseases), John Singleton, who dedicated his life to the moral and physical reform of the underprivileged and oppressed, James Jamison (both in relation to infant mortality), and J.T. Rudall, particularly in the field of ophthalmology, are noteworthy. R.A. Stirling was interested in *morbus coxae,* a field in which P.B. Bennie was later to become prominent. The early work of W. Gillbee and G.H. Pringle on the introduction of Listerism included child cases. The variety of William Snowball's paediatric contributions from Melbourne in the latter decades of the century is impressive. So too is the work of A.J. Turner, from Brisbane, and A.J. Wood in Melbourne, whose interests were similar in that both published papers on diphtheria antitoxin and intubation in the 1890s, and both were later concerned with infant feeding and welfare. With E.A. Mackay, Wood was responsible for the preparation of abstracts from overseas publications on paediatric subjects which began to appear regularly towards the end of the century. J.W. Springthorpe was interested particularly in epilepsy, and R.R.S. Stawell wrote on a variety of paediatric subjects; both were primarily general physicians. On the surgical side, G.A. Syme, a pioneer in appendicectomy, ranged over a wide field, while W. Moore and Hamilton Russell, with others, began to take a particular interest in congenital malformations, notably hare lip, cleft palate, hernia and external genito-urinary malformations, as surgical techniques became better developed. W. Kent-Hughes was a pioneer in the orthopaedic field, and an innovator in the treatment of clubfoot; C.P.B. Clubbe adopted his operation in Sydney, and also corrected bow legs. As might be expected of a man whose interests remained extraordinarily wide throughout his life, J.W. (later Sir James) Barrett wrote extensively on medical and surgical paediatric topics, with an obviously developing interest in eye, ear, nose and throat conditions. A.W. Finch Noyes showed dermatological cases of paediatric interest at meetings of the Medical Society of Victoria, where there were also regular contributions relating to childhood pathology by H.B. Allen and C.H. Mollison.

In 1896 F.J. Clendinnen, a pioneer in Australian radiology, was able to show a skiagram of a child's ankylosed elbow joint. Localisation of foreign bodies in the oesophagus by this method was reported by Syme three years later, but the most remarkable case was described in 1903. The position of a pin in the left lower lobe bronchus was accurately localised by radiography in two planes at right angles by W.R. Fox, and this enabled Hamilton Russell to plan a deft removal at thoracotomy with open anaesthesia; this must be one of the first cases of lung surgery in children. J. Davies Thomas in 1889 drew attention to the increasing prevalence of hydatid disease since the middle of the century; perhaps 20% of fatal cases involved people under the age of 20 years. The mortality in childhood, never very high, declined only after this period. Davies Thomas' classic monograph on this disease was published in Adelaide in 1894; it was neither the first nor the last Australian contribution to knowledge of this condition.

The pioneers of the appendicectomy in Australia were Syme and Clubbe but their respective mortality rates of 25% and 16% in the closing years of the nineteenth century must have been disturbingly close to the mortality without surgical intervention; they doubtless reflect the fact that surgery was usually undertaken in severe cases, at a relatively late stage, and in the presence of complications. Controversy over the selection of cases for surgery, and the role of interval surgery, continued for many years.

Perhaps the major surgical issue of the late nineteenth century was the management of intussusception. Variations on the theme of hydrostatic reduction were in vogue, but Clubbe, at the Royal Alexandra Hospital for Children, advocated surgical intervention, as in his hands less than 10% were reduced by the hydrostatic method. Clubbe wrote an important monograph on the subject in 1907, with a second edition in 1921; in the later series his operative mortality was 25%. Somewhat later, at the same hospital, P.L. Hipsley refined the hydrostatic method, notably by using radio-opaque material so that the result could be observed radiographically.

The *Australasian Medical Gazette* covered a very similar range of material. Two additional subjects raised were the problems of spider bites and of childhood rickets; the latter was probably associated with the introduction of artificial foods and processed milk products, expensive but widely used by the 1880s. G. Lane Mullens contributed historical papers, including a valuable account of the history of vaccination in Australia. H.C. Hinder wrote on surgical subjects, notably appendicitis. J. Stapleton, who had published a textbook of neurology in London, discussed intracranial tumours, and Spencer Gillies presented a paper on cerebrospinal meningitis. C.A. Altman reported 12 cases of poliomyelitis from South Australia in 1897. Alexander Francis, of Brisbane, wrote on adenoids in 1899; he was later to publish a book on asthma in relation to the nose (1903) and to describe 'Francis' triad' (nasal polypi, asthma and aspirin sensitivity). One of the most important papers was a careful review by C.P.B. Clubbe and W.F. Litchfield in 1896 on the use of the new diphtheria antitoxin; it is interesting that they also used trypsin to dissolve or loosen the diphtheritic membrane. Among others to demonstrate a paediatric interest were A.E. Mills, R. Scot Skirving, of Sydney, and A.A. Lendon of Adelaide.

Perhaps the most famous names in paediatrics of this period were A.J. Turner and A.J. Wood. Turner was the first in Brisbane to describe meningococcal meningitis, and with J. Lockhart Gibson he first described ankylostomiasis in Australian children; the ova were demonstrated in the faeces of children with anaemia. Turner worked with Behring shortly after the latter had developed diphtheria antitoxin, and Turner was amongst the first to use it in this country. Gibson and Turner also described lead poisoning in children, the diagnosis being first made early in 1890 and first described in two classical papers in 1892 and 1897. Various manifestations were recognised, and Gibson was responsible for describing ocular neuritis due to lead. Gibson himself described the problems of identifying the source of the lead, but in 1904 he collected paint from his own verandah, in which large amounts of lead were found. With Lucy Gullett, he then proceeded to establish that most of the victims of lead poisoning were nail biters and finger suckers. Turner was later to record his disillusion with politicians, administrators, and vested interests in the course of a long and difficult campaign to control the use of lead in paints. He attributed the eventual success in controlling the disease not so much to legislative action as to 'the education of the public and the discovery by the painting trade that non-poisonous paints on surfaces exposed to weathering age just as well'. In fact it was not until 1923 that regulations previously gazetted were satisfactorily enforced. Turner was one of many at the turn of the century to emphasise the value of breast feeding, which in his view the profession did not stress sufficiently to the public. As a result, he became a leading figure in infant welfare movements in Brisbane. He advocated fresh milk as a substitute for breast feeding, and this necessitated his giving attention to ensuring a supply of fresh, pure milk. He realised that contamination could readily occur in the home, and he advocated scalding the milk as soon as it was received. He was concerned with the establishment of pasteurization of milk and with arranging supplies of ice so that milk could be kept cool in the home.

Adaptation to the tropics, both by children and by adults, was for many years a matter of contention. The ability of Europeans to live, work and reproduce in the tropics was not finally accepted until the 1930s. Gordon, using infant mortality rates as an index of adaptation, showed that in the decade centred on 1880 the rate for Brisbane was 180 per 1,000, for tropical Queensland 140 and for the settled farming area of the Darling Downs 106. All three rates progressively declined, so that in the decade centred on 1910 the rates were 90, 64 and 63.

Plumbism was later implicated in the high mortality of young people from chronic nephritis in Queensland by D.G. Croll and L.J.J. Nye in 1929, a problem which is still not fully resolved. Other Queensland problems were malaria in the northern area during the nineteenth century, and filariasis, possibly introduced with the Kanaka labour force, which was identified in about 5% of children in Brisbane and subsequently in the coastal strip. At a later period, Harvey Sutton estimated that 75% of school children in Queensland had had dengue. Queensland was also the unfortunate site of the Bundaberg tragedy in 1928, when 12 children lost their lives from staphylococcal septicaemia following diphtheria immunisation.

Perhaps inevitably, Wood's interests were similar to those of Turner. He learned the O'Dwyer technique of intubation for laryngeal diphtheria whilst overseas and was probably the first to use it in Australia. He was also one of the first in this country to demonstrate that cretinism could be improved by oral thyroid. Like Turner, Wood became deeply involved in the problems of infant feeding and directed much effort towards improving the quality of the milk supply; he advocated fresh milk as a substitute for breast feeding but was opposed to its being boiled because he believed that this predisposed to infantile scurvy.

When pink disease or erythroedema was first described by Swift, of Adelaide, in 1914, Wood and F. Hobill Cole were able to produce a retrospective series of nearly 100 cases dating back to the 1890s. It is possible that Clubbe, who recognised the disease about the same time, introduced the term 'pink disease'. Many years later, in 1935, Wood published a further study with his son, I.J. Wood, who had translated C. Rocaz' minor classic on this disease in 1933. Sir Ian Wood drew my attention to the treatment of one patient diagnosed in 1898 with a mercurial binder, in spite of which he recovered. The disease disappeared in the last two or three decades with the prohibition of mercury in teething powders, although its decline antedated legislative enactments.

This summary review of published work in paediatrics indicates that by the first decade of the twentieth century an increasing awareness of childhood problems had led to local publications over almost the whole range of medicine and surgery. At the same time, it illustrates the gradual evolution of specialisation in paediatrics with the emergence of men such as Turner and Wood, although probably very few could rely solely on childhood practice. Childhood diseases were an important part of general practice, and the spirit of self-reliance, which was already a part of the tradition of the Australian general practitioner, was probably not conducive to widespread consultative practice, even if it had been acceptable to the majority of patients. Many doctors of consultant status practised both medicine and surgery; perhaps in paediatrics this was to persist a little longer than in adult medicine. The development of specialisation was facilitated by the establishment of children's hospitals, for the most part in the last quarter of the nineteenth century (Appendix I); many of the persons named had affiliations with these institutions. Finally, the review indicates that many specialties, notably ophthalmology and otorhinolaryngology, were taking notice of the particular problems of children. Indeed, children, excellent patients for several reasons, may well have benefitted more than adults from the early advances of modern medicine.

References and further reading

Simpson, S. & Tovell, A. A bibliography of Australian paediatrics 1846-1900. *Australian Paediatric Journal,* 1978, in the press.

12 CHARITABLE AND INSTITUTIONAL DEVELOPMENTS FROM 1850

> Thank God, some of the heartless brutes who
> thought flogging three times a day and solitary
> confinement on bread and water, moral and medical
> treatment for the physical weakness of 'wetting
> the bed' are no longer in power.

> E.S. Hall, *Aust. Med. J.*, 1860

> The State upon the Home I planned —
> Yea, for it built the State.

> Bernard O'Dowd, *Juno,* 1907

In New South Wales, responsibility for the orphan schools passed essentially from government to church in 1826, additional funds being granted for the establishment of Catholic orphan schools in 1836. The Governor acquired power to apprentice these children in 1834, and about 30 boys each year were apprenticed under this scheme to 1839; the boys were much in demand, but the girls less so. Governor Darling's wife established a Female School of Industry in 1826 for girls from the age of 7 years, 20 being admitted initially. At 14 they were placed in employment, preference being given to subscribers to the institution.

By the 1850s the scope of the social welfare activities of the Benevolent Society of New South Wales was virtually all-embracing. It had established some outdoor relief in 1818, and opened its asylum (1821) and the Sydney Dispensary (1826); it undertook other responsibilities. Its finances came from private subscription and from government support for special projects. As some 60% of its income was ultimately derived from England, it was apparent that increasing independence of the colony would require reappraisal of the structure of social welfare services, and an inquiry began in 1854. In appointing the board, the Colonial Secretary expressed certain prevailing attitudes: a lying-in hospital was an evil because it encouraged the abandoned to procreate and offered no check to immoral conduct. Similarly, a foundling hospital was an evil if it induced parents to abandon their children.

Understandably, progress was slow in such an environment, although a Select Committee was appointed to report on the Benevolent Society and its role in 1861. The Society accepted some responsibility for destitute children at that time, and the report noted that 63 children in a ward all bathed in the same tub of water, and eight of them slept in one bed. These findings may be compared with those of the 1854 inquiry, where it emerged that children in the orphan schools slept in their day clothes which were changed weekly. On the other hand, between 1850 and 1858 inclusive 1,725 children under 12 years of age were admitted with a mortality overall of only 6%; among 374 infants under 12 months 68 (18%) died, even though 80% of the latter had been nursed by their mothers. In 1862 the government took over responsibility for the aged and infirm, the Benevolent Society being requested to continue to look after expectant mothers, women with infants and the younger poor children; some government finance was provided for these purposes. By 1866, when some legislative control over public charities was introduced, there were the Protestant and Catholic orphanages catering for approximately 500 children, the Female School of Industry, the Randwick Asylum (for children other than infants) (Chapter 13), and a small Hebrew society established in 1833 concerned with Jewish orphans. Three 'ragged schools' conducted by voluntary efforts had been functioning in the poorer areas of Sydney since 1860; the salaried teachers offered some opportunity for free education to neglected youngsters, and they appear to have had sufficient interest in their welfare to visit their homes and learn their backgrounds. Evening classes were conducted, and a total of nearly 500 were soon under instruction. The Lisgard Training School, which provided aid for young girls who appeared in court for any reason, may be added, although it did not open until 1870; about 20 girls aged 8 to 11 years were given instruction in household duties and elementary education.

As a sequel to the population increase and socio-economic stresses of the gold rushes there were many neglected children or 'orphans' by 1866, when Henry Parkes successfully introduced a number of bills concerned with social welfare. Industrial schools were established for children under 12 years of age who were beggars, vagrants, associating with undesirable companions or found sleeping without a home. After the age of 12 these children could be formally apprenticed on government authority. Juvenile reformatories were also established, notably on the ship *Vernon*, where over 100 children were soon established. The distinction between reformatory and industrial schools (essentially a court conviction) was not always maintained.

Common to all states were two problems which increasingly harassed the legislature and troubled the public conscience over the next decades. The first was concern as to the frequency of infanticide, and the second related to the adverse psychological effects of 'institutionalising' children in relatively large numbers.

Infanticide was probably never absent from a society in which extreme pressures were placed upon young unmarried mothers, and the 'battered baby syndrome' is likely to be as old as civilization. The *Colonial Observer*'s concern about secret interments of children in 1841 is probably not an isolated comment; the practice of baby-farming must inevitably have grown from advertisements for wet nurses which may be traced back to the early years of the *Sydney* and *Hobart Gazettes.* Probably few of these were medically supervised, although in 1860 one advertisement directed applicants to contact a medical practitioner. Infanticide excited concern in a Melbourne medical journal in 1863, where in about 25% of inquests on children under 3 years of age death could be attributed to causes denoting neglect, ignorance or maltreatment, and this pattern continued into the 1870s. Nonetheless, juries were reluctant to bring a verdict of infanticide against mothers. Public concern led to the establishment by private charity of the Sydney Foundling Hospital, opened at Darlinghurst in 1874 but soon transferred to Ashfield as the Infants' Home when a suitable house was provided by its honorary medical officer, Dr. C.F. Fischer. The Victorian Infant Asylum was established in Fitzroy in 1877 with the alleviation of infanticide and reduction in the mortality of illegitimate infants as its major objectives. Medical aspects of these early paediatric institutions are examined in Chapter 13. A small Female Mission Home, also established in Sydney in 1873, initially admitted 12 mothers and their babies. By its third year the Sydney Foundling Hospital and Home for Destitute Infants congratulated itself on 'tending to prevent infanticide, and to alleviate much social misery', whilst of its Victorian counterpart it was said that without its aid some of the children 'would certainly have been murdered, while others would surely have died of neglect'. By the 1880s the Benevolent Society was giving much aid to mothers trying to earn their own living and thus to look after their own children, a different approach to the same problem.

The social tragedy of infanticide was expressed by J.S. Nielson in a horrifying poem, *Marian's Child,* which was omitted from his collected works:

> Why should it live to plague us?
> Why should it ever begin
> Travelling roads of trouble,
> Soiling its soul with sin? ...
>
> Down at the foot of the garden,
> Where the moon-made shadows fall,
> I sold myself to the devil
> And bought a home in hell.

These measures reflect a radical change in outlook over a mere two decades, but institutions of this kind were in themselves not a sufficient answer. In the 1890s extreme instances of baby-farming were brought to light. In Sydney in 1892, Mr. and Mrs. Makin were found to have buried a number of babies in the gardens of several houses which they had occupied. Their technique was to advertise under various names, representing themselves as fond parents anxious to give affection to some unwanted baby. Their activities were revealed because some of the mothers became too persistent in wanting to see their infants. An unqualified midwife at Lane Cove, also a professional baby farmer, certified that she delivered a woman of a premature male child, on which statement the child was buried as 'stillborn', although it was in fact two months old. In Melbourne in 1894 Frances Knorr was hanged for killing one child; she confessed to killing two and was suspected of disposing of a dozen. These cases precipitated legislation in New South Wales and Victoria — indeed, in all states — to register and inspect all foster homes, to supervise all young children placed in foster care by parents or relations and to improve the system of medical certification of infant deaths.

The second problem arose from widely expressed criticisms that the large institutions, such as orphanages and industrial schools, 'depersonalised' the children and deprived them of affection and the moral and religious background assumed to be available in most respectable homes. While these views may be accepted as true on *a priori* grounds, especially as suitable staff were not always available in sufficient numbers, it is difficult to assess in retrospect just how psychologically ineffectual or deleterious these institutions were. There are reliable accounts of the Randwick Asylum and the industrial schools which indicate that the children were happy, healthy and well-supervised, and some of these came from noted medical practitioners capable of critical evaluation. On the other hand, there are descriptions of dull and apathetic children, treated as almost less than human by disinterested staff; at least two doctors referred 'to the entire loss of individuality by the children being massed together'. Criticism was strongest in Hobart, and an extreme example is quoted at the head of this chapter. What is certain is that much depended on the person in charge, and there was therefore probably wide variation between institutions and from time to time. The *Vernon,* for example, appears to have been successful but its female counterpart at Newcastle was not. The successful outcome, as judged by follow-up of child inmates after their apprenticeship, is well documented in the case of the Randwick Asylum, and appears to justify the view that these institutions did 'convert many waifs and strays into useful colonists'. As outlined in Chapter 13, medical supervision appears to have been as good as contemporary knowledge allowed, and considerable pride was taken by lay and medical staff in maintaining a good health record.

Royal Commissions in New South Wales (1873-74) and Victoria (1872) were critical of these institutions, and at this period the move towards adopting the 'boarding-out system', at least for orphans and destitute children, gained momentum. This system is usually said to have been introduced first in South Australia in 1872, although it was employed on a limited but increasing scale in Hobart after 1871. In Adelaide at this time a Boarding-Out Society was established by a voluntary charitable group of ladies and it immediately received some government subsidy. One of the founders subsequently took the initiative in starting a similar society in Sydney in 1879, while a third was formed under the auspices of the Presbyterian Church in Melbourne in 1872. The principle of the boarding-out system appealed to governments whose institutional systems were under criticism, and within a few years boarding-out

Plate 1. Then and now. The stone Catherine Hayes Hospital (1870) has a forbidding appearance which contrasts with the open design of the new Prince of Wales Children's Hospital. The old building is still to be seen facing Avoca Street in the grounds of the Prince of Wales Hospital. (J. Coulter, *Randwick Asylum: an historical review of the Society for the Relief of Destitute Children from the year 1852 up to ... 1915,* and Department of Medical Illustration, University of New South Wales.)

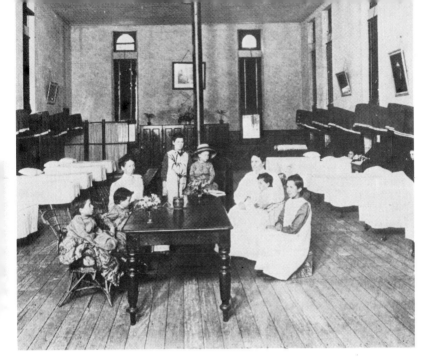

Plate 2. Then and now. The interior of the girls' ward in the Catherine Hayes Hospital is austere; it shows nine children (three in bed) in the care of two nurses. A more relaxed atmosphere pervades the play area of the new Children's Hospital. (J. Coulter, *Randwick Asylum: an historical review of the Society for the Relief of Destitute Children from the year 1852 up to ... 1915,* and Department of Medical Illustration, University of New South Wales.)

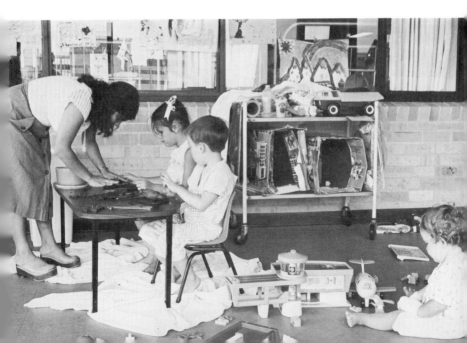

was legislatively established as government policy (for example, by 1881 in New South Wales and 1874 in Victoria). This was implemented usually by government and voluntary organisations assuming responsibility jointly; the administration was cumbersome, relying on supervision by honorary volunteers, but it seems to have worked successfully. The guardians were carefully selected, and care was taken to ensure that the children were adequately housed and given reasonable opportunities both in work and education. A subsidy was payable to the host family but at least in South Australia many families did not seek it. In New South Wales the subsidy was higher for delicate children, and higher still for sick or disabled ones.

The acceptance by all parties of the boarding-out system is surprising in its enthusiasm. In all states the homes for destitute children and orphans were virtually emptied within a decade. I am aware of no detailed comments which were critical of the scheme, and even that faintly cynical observer of the Melbourne scene, 'The Vagabond' (Julian Thomas) wrote appreciatively of it after conducting one of his personal investigations. Some problems arose when parents wanted their children back, and this probably gave impetus to the introduction of legislation to permit legal adoption, first accepted by Western Australia in 1896. This year also saw the introduction in New South Wales of a scheme whereby a deserving widow or deserted wife could have her own child boarded out to herself; many children thus returned to their mothers.

There was one cautiously discordant note amidst the praise for the boarding-out system. W.F. Litchfield, in the *Australasian Medical Gazette* for 1899, estimated that a minimum of 52% of infants boarded out under the age of six months died. In his view, this was only a small improvement on the mortality in foundling homes where artificial feeding was the rule, and not as good as could be achieved in institutions which insisted on breast feeding. I know of no other studies of this kind, but it may have been that the system contributed more to the psychological welfare of older children than it did to a lessening of infant mortality. Incidentally, provision for obtaining medical care from local practitioners was usually included in the arrangements made for boarding children out.

The social background of children to whom the boarding-out system meant so much may be gauged from the experience of the New South Wales State Children's Relief Board. Of the 5,700 children boarded out prior to 1898, both parents were dead in only 13%, 37% were children whose mother was destitute with father dead or deserted, while the mother was dead and father had deserted or was unemployed in a further 13%; a variety of unfortunate circumstances accounted for the remainder. Victorian authorities were at first cautious in boarding out primarily children under 8 years, because they had often become 'difficult' by the age of 9, and by 12 they were well aware of their rights under the apprentice or license systems. Some governments, as in Tasmania from 1867, tended to retain direct control over all delinquent or 'criminal' children. The distinction, both in Tasmania and elsewhere, was not always clear, and depended in part on the attitude of children's courts, established as a rule about the turn of the century. Even if only because of the reduced responsibility of the states for all neglected children, the lot of this disadvantaged group gradually improved.

In Tasmania, the social circumstances of the colony meant that the government had always made a major financial contribution to private charitable enterprises. In 1867 the government passed legislation which effectively encouraged the establishment of industrial schools by voluntary agencies, in effect the churches, but even when government was mainly responsible financially for an institution it commonly sought the aid of visiting committees, honorary boards, or voluntary service in some way. This dual responsibility was conducive to conflict, but it may also have contributed to the early adoption of the boarding-out system. Following the establishment of a boys' reformatory in the 1870s, and of a boys' training school in 1884, the secretary of the latter indicated that his main aims were to create a home influence, to allow as much freedom as possible, to avoid corporal punishment and 'to arouse good moral tone' — views doubtless conditioned by the criticisms of institutional management and the success of boarding-out. A similar institution was opened for girls in 1881, but the occupancy of all had greatly diminished by 1900. By this time, all states had child welfare services more or less at a similar stage of evolution, although the change from voluntary to state agencies had been less dramatic in Tasmania than elsewhere.

In Western Australia, features of interest were an ordinance of 1842 appointing a guardian of the 'juvenile immigrants' (drawn from British penal institutions) and the establishment in 1882 of a reformatory on Rottnest Island for children who would previously have been imprisoned. The details of legislation and charitable care were otherwise generally similar to the progress outlined above chiefly in relation to New South Wales.

There were of course many other organisations, often small, whose aid, directly or indirectly, implied benefits for children. One of the largest and most influential of these was the Immigrants' Aid Society in Melbourne, formed in the gold rush era. It cared for deserted children, with government aid, from 1857 until 1864 when this segment of its activities was transferred to the government following legislation under which the government assumed responsibility for neglected children and established its own industrial schools. By the same act, incidentally, a reform school was established on the hulk *Deborah*. The Society also maintained a conventional school in its home for immigrants. The St. James Dorcas Society, founded in 1845, took over in 1850 a small orphanage previously conducted through the private philanthropy of one of its members, an institution destined to become the Melbourne Orphans' Asylum in 1854.

These examples, taken almost at random, must serve to

illustrate the contribution made by voluntary charitable groups to child welfare before the several states assumed the major responsibility. As a generalisation, the transitional period 1850-1900 was often one of some administrative uncertainty, and even recurrent crises, while governments believed that community self-help should be encouraged and voluntary agencies depended on an often capricious subsidy. In this transitional phase there was also often the dual system of control, part governmental, part voluntary, which, in spite of some apparent advantages, did not make for harmony and efficiency. In evaluating institutional care as the first major intrusion of the state into child welfare, it must be remembered that the new colonial governments, legislatively and socially inexperienced, and often unstable, were confronted with a massive problem at the beginning of the period. This is not to deny a gradual change in social attitudes, particularly towards unmarried mothers and their children. As usual, the poets, often militant social critics at the turn of the century, became involved, and a medical practitioner wrote scathingly of the Women's Hospital, Melbourne:

'Sorry, can't admit you',
  Decency declines
To tolerate a mother
  Without 'marriage lines'.

A.M. Hill, *Marriage Lines,* 1899

By the time of the depressions of the 1890s and the more slowly evolving problems associated with the drift of the population to the towns the outlook for the 'stunted children ... in squalid lanes and alleys black' (A.B. Paterson) was improving, legislatively and materially.

These considerations perhaps justify a brief review of child welfare in a broader perspective as the early years of the present century unfolded. The most persistent advocate of progress in child welfare measures in any state was C.K. Mackellar, born in Sydney, and a medical graduate of Glasgow in 1871, who devoted much of his life to politics and the administration of the State Children's Relief Department. Some of his arguments might not be acceptable in principle today, as when he advocated the state's taking over the children of living but dissolute or idle parents on the grounds that the boarding-out of orphans had been so successful, but his aim was always the welfare of the child, primarily as a human being and only secondarily as an investment in the national future. From the 1890s he, like others, had been concerned that the mortality rate for illegitimate children was about three times that of the legitimate; in 1913, he criticised women, who, enfranchised in 1902, had failed to compel their political representatives 'to give consideration to a matter which is of vital interest to their sex'. Mackellar recognised the need for mentally retarded or deficient children to be treated differently from those who were merely destitute or neglected. He appreciated that the children's courts, admirable in principle, could produce anomalies in management when they had the option of referring the children to a variety of different institutions or of having them boarded out in the same way as orphans; he knew that magistrates were reluctant to draw a distinction between the destitute, the immoral, the delinquent or the criminal. Reviewing progress in social welfare over several decades, he regarded it as 'curious' that 'while its initiation most frequently depends upon the philanthropic enterprise of private individuals, its development rests ultimately with the State'.

This shift in emphasis from private to state responsibility has rightly been regarded as a striking feature of the late nineteenth century attitudes. The trend has been considered one of reform, but the process is, I believe, more accurately depicted as one of evolution than revolution. Social historians often imply that the earlier institutions were a mistake, based presumably on the notion that our forebears should have had the wisdom, insight and understanding vouchsafed to an enlightened mid-twentieth century community, and also on the conviction that today's standards are both absolute and right. This ignores the possibility that modern society is not so senescent that its present views are immutable; I believe, indeed I hope, that they will change. In the light of medical considerations, it seems more realistic to adopt the view that the children were physically, perhaps even psychologically, better off in the institutional environment than in the conditions from which they came (as set out, for example, in the report of the Select Committee on the conditions of the working classes in Sydney in 1860). This view implies that any concept of welfare is relative, or even that there can be no absolute standard. The logical and inevitable approach was to gather the waifs and strays together, not unsuccessfully by the standards of the time, and thereafter it became possible to consider alternative schemes. The success generally conceded to the apprenticeship which followed institutional upbringing gave some confidence to legislators anxious to introduce boarding-out, similar in principle but applying at an earlier age, and not in widespread use overseas at the time institutions such as the Randwick Asylum and the industrial schools were established. The transfer of responsibility from voluntary agencies and private support to government control and sponsorship may be viewed partly as reflecting a change in society's attitudes but also as a manifestation of the Australian propensity for disposing of any possible responsibility to governmental authority, an antipodean characteristic apparent in many fields besides welfare.

In 1917, Mackellar severely criticised the 'Baby Bonus Act' of the Federal Government (1912), on grounds which make interesting reading today. In effect, any woman having a live, but not a stillborn, baby acquired a maternity allowance of £5. Mackellar averred that the government's excellent intention was to aid the less well-to-do, but that it was frightened to say so for fear of being accused of class legislation; in modern terms, no means test was applied. He argued forcefully that more good could be done, at the same cost, by providing accommodation for half the country's mothers for a few weeks before and after confinement, and he supplied both the results of experience and the necessary calculations. A politician relying on such simple but realistic logic today would scarcely survive, but whether this implies further reform in social attitudes, or evolution, or the kind of dependent regression suggested in the previous paragraph it may be premature to judge. Child endowment, subject to a means test, was introduced in New South Wales in 1927 and by the Federal Government as a generally available benefit in 1941; the payroll tax was developed to provide the required revenue.

References and further reading

Bignell, S. Orphans and destitute children in Victoria up to 1864. *Victorian Historical Magazine,* 1973, 44: 5.

Dickey, B. The establishment of industrial schools and reformatories in New South Wales 1850-1875. *Journal of the Royal Australian Historical Society,* 1968, 54: 135.

Dickey, B. Care for deprived, neglected and delinquent children in New South Wales, 1901-1915. *Journal of the Royal Australian Historical Society,* 1977, 63: 167.

Mackellar, C.K. *The child, the law, and the state.* Sydney, 1907.

Peyser, D. A study of the history of welfare work in Sydney from 1788 till about 1900. *Journal of the Royal Australian Historical Society,* 1939, 25: 89, 169.

13 MEDICAL ASPECTS OF INSTITUTIONAL CARE

In the long row your little grave
    Can cover all your baby fears.
The great world cursed you and you died
    Dear little unloved child of tears.

J.S. Nielson, *Child of Tears, c.* 1920

The institutional care described in Chapter 12 which characterised the organisation of child welfare services prior to the last decade or two of the nineteenth century may now be examined chiefly from a medical viewpoint. These institutions antedated the conventional children's hospitals which were developing and which are still in existence; they were, in effect, the paediatric hospitals of a slightly earlier period. As illustrative examples, we shall examine the Ashfield Infants' Home in Sydney, a Melbourne orphanage, the Randwick Asylum, Sydney, and the Victorian industrial schools, each for a short period.

The Infants' Home, Ashfield, opened in 1874, had, by the time of its third annual report, extended its scope to include the infants of married people when one or other parent was deceased or had deserted. There had been 61 applications for admission, of which 31 were accepted. The reasons for refusal, other than ineligibility or want of room, were the prevalence of a local epidemic (leading to refusal of all admissions) and lack of wet nurses when the mothers declined admission with the child. Eleven children had been left at the door of the hospital, while 9 were admitted with their mothers. The mortality was only about 52%, which was 'a matter of astonishment' in view of the current typhoid and gastroenteritis epidemics, and the poor state of health and nourishment of many of the children on admission. Many had come from untrustworthy nurses to whom the mothers had paid a regular sum for the maintenance of the child, a reflection of the practice of baby farming. Often the mothers had not had an adequate supply of breast milk, so that the baby had been 'dry nursed' prior to admission. In these cases the same system was continued in the hospital, using milk from the institution's own cow. If the applicant was nursing her child and there was no available wet nurse, then both mother and baby were admitted, a practice which it seems was not followed if a wet nurse was available. However 'in no single case is a young baby admitted and the style of its nursing changed'. Gastrointestinal disorders caused two-thirds of the deaths. Seven children were admitted 'in a hopeless state', 12 were poor and emaciated, 13 had a scrofulous constitution and only 10 were 'in a healthy state'. According to the medical report, deaths seem to have been distributed evenly between those who were dry nursed and those who were wet nursed.

By 1879, some parents were contributing a small sum in proportion to their earnings towards the support of their children, thus freeing a single parent to be gainfully employed. During the year, 121 children had been admitted and there had been only 19 deaths; 12 had been admitted moribund. Further evidence of improved management with experience is indicated by a lower mortality amongst the children who were partially or wholly wet nursed by comparison with those who were 'hand-fed'; the mortality rates were 11% as against 44% of those dry nursed. This result was achieved in spite of the fact that the mothers were often reluctant nurses not in good health; usually they had two infants to care for at the same time.

The commonest diseases encountered were gastrointestinal disorders and ophthalmia. The medical officer congratulated himself on the excellent results of his homeopathic treatment of ophthalmia by frequent cleansing with warm water; although there were some purulent cases, and some with keratitis or corneal ulceration, all completely recovered, in spite of the crowded conditions and the unsatisfactory general health of many of the patients. He also commented that many of the women were in a state of health which made them unfit to nurse their own infants and, even more, unfit to have an additional infant given to them; some said that they had been inadequately fed at the Benevolent Society after they had given birth to their children under its care. In 1876 the hospital congratulated itself on keeping the acute infectious diseases, such as scarlet fever and measles, out of the institution, although there had been deaths in the neighbourhood.

The experience of the Protestant Orphan Asylum at Emerald Hill in Melbourne was different. From 1850 to 1859 there were only 28 deaths, mostly amongst children admitted moribund, although the average daily occupancy had increased from 30 in 1854 to 136 by 1859. E.S. Hall was probably right in claiming that this mortality experience was less than in the Hobart institutions, although he exaggerated the difference. Over 21 months 1859-1862, there were only 7 deaths, including two infants who died from dysentery and infantile convulsions. The average daily occupancy was about 150, and the total population at risk was 229, but it is difficult to evaluate the significance of the low mortality in the absence of a knowledge of age distribution. Certainly infants under 1 year appear in the list of deaths, the causes of which were varied. The institution was not able to escape epidemic disease. In one month there were 30 cases of scarlet fever, with one death, while on another occasion there were 70 cases of measles, nearly half the inmates, without a death. According to F.T. West Ford, the surgeon, the figures showed 'that infant life is not so precarious as some would lead us to believe', and he referred to a widely held view that Australia had 'the reputation of being dangerous to children', a misconception 'which must have a very prejudicial effect upon its interests, preventing numbers from permanently settling, who might otherwise do so'.

In 1852 the Society for the Relief of Destitute Children was established in Sydney with the object of assisting children who were foundlings, abandoned or vagrant, or born of dissolute parents, together with children with one responsible parent unable to provide for a child. It aimed to provide not merely protection and support but also industrial training and moral and religious instruction. A leading figure in its establishment was Dr. H.G. Douglass who, in spite of a reputation for harshness as a magistrate in the penal period some 30 years earlier, had become one of a group of citizens prominent in a variety of charitable and philanthropic organisations. The Asylum opened in a house in Paddington, but largely as a result of a generous bequest by its first honorary medical officer, Dr. Alexander Cuthill, it was transferred to a commodious building, planned to house 400 children, on the Randwick site in March 1858. In 1859 all the children were vaccinated, a wise precaution. Within a decade an additional wing was required for a further 400 children. With such a large child population, the need for a hospital was quickly appreciated, especially after a measles epidemic in 1860 (113 cases with no deaths). The earlier generosity of the Irish soprano, Catherine Hayes, enabled the erection of the building named after her in 1870, now, after various vicissitudes, the psychiatric unit of the Prince of Wales Hospital. In a sense, the hospital came too late, for in 1867 an epidemic of whooping cough, together with measles (both causing high mortality in Sydney generally at the time) caused no less than 77 deaths, probably about 10% of the children in the institution. The complications included bronchitis, diarrhoea and dysentery, convulsions and 'secondary fever', and they affected chiefly 'the youngest and most delicate'. Some typhoid fever was prevalent later in the year, and ophthalmia also became epidemic.

The devastating impact of an institutional epidemic is indicated by the fact that the 1867 epidemic lasted only about two months; at any one time perhaps 200 children may have been ill. The mortality was the highest from which the institution had suffered in its 15 years of existence; usually annual deaths were below 1% of the population at any one time. The opening of the hospital, with its 'additional facilities as to separation, nursing, bathing appliances, &c.', was found to meet the objects for which it was intended and doubtless played a part in the subsequently low mortality. There were only two deaths in its first year, probably an average figure up to the 1880s, and by 1914 it could be recorded that only four children had died in the previous 26 years. A few years after the Catherine Hayes Hospital was opened a receiving house was built to isolate and treat children who were admitted suffering from contagious or infectious diseases; the almost universal ophthalmia of 1878-79 had stressed the need for an establishment of this kind. A convalescent home was also founded near Campbelltown.

The age distribution of children in the institution in 1873 was as follows: 4% under the age of 5 years (the Asylum did not admit infants, and rarely children under 4), 27% aged 5 to 7 years, 32% from 7 to 9 years, 28% aged 9 to 11 years and 8% up to 13 years. Some schooling was provided, and from 1877 this was incorporated in the state educational system. An apprenticeship scheme was operative after the age of 12, and it was said that 'in nearly all cases the children turned out well', although appropriate precautions were taken to prevent abuse. Efforts were made to keep in touch with these children, if only by correspondence.

A farm was maintained at Randwick (at a later stage the cows which provided the milk had to be destroyed because of tuberculosis) and the boys worked in this as well as at a variety of trades, whilst the girls were trained in the usual domestic duties. The water supply was a recurring difficulty in earlier years, and both tanks and wells were employed. The contents of sewage pits were daily used for manure.

In 1876 a board of inquiry was critical of some aspects of the Asylum's conduct, notably staff inadequacy, the impersonal nature of the supervision and the recreational facilities. There was also an unfortunate sectarian dispute, for the Asylum was non-sectarian in its origin and practice. Probably the institution had simply grown too big. However, in 1883 the boarding-out system for destitute children was introduced in New South Wales, and by 1886 there were only 250 children left in the Asylum. As this led to a substantial loss of income from the government, it was a disaster for the institution. Despite the shortage of funds, the annual report for 1894 mentions, surprisingly, that research on the prevention of disease had included bacteriological studies by Dr. Frank Tidswell, later the director of the Bureau of Microbiology for the New South Wales Government, 'in his private laboratory', apparently without cost to the institution; unfortunately no details are available. By this time there were only about 150 inmates with about 50 admissions yearly and about 20 in the hospital at any one time. The depression of the 1890s added to the financial problems, and led to reductions in staff and salaries, and to rejection of some children commended for admission.

By the first world war, it is probable that the institution as constituted had outlived its usefulness, but it came as a shock when the New South Wales Government suddenly introduced legislation to take over an entire charitable organisation. The buildings, some of which had already been offered by the Society to the Federal Government to house wounded or disabled returned servicemen, were eventually all used for this purpose, and it was not for half a century that children's wards were again opened on the site as part of the newly developed Prince of Wales Hospital. Although not a lineal descendant of the old Randwick Asylum, today's Children's Hospital (opened in 1977) may care to accept the honourable tradition of its predecessor. On its closure in 1915, the Asylum proudly recorded that it had cared for nearly 6,000 children, of whom 300 had been apprenticed, 2,800 returned to parents or discharged, and only 216, or 3.7% of the total, had died while in the Society's care.

Some insight into the medical and logistic problems confronting the industrial schools is provided by a review of the first years of their establishment in Victoria. In August 1864, when the Neglected and Criminal Children's Act came into operation, 463 children were transferred from the care of the Immigrants' Aid Society. In addition, during the year 190 children were committed from various police courts in the colony. There were 10 deaths, 49 discharges and 4 absconders, leaving 590 children in the schools at the end of 1864. During 1865, 868 children were received. There were 117 deaths, 73 discharges to the naval training ship, 13 to orphanages, 3 children were licensed out as servants, 4 absconded and 162 were discharged, leaving 1,095 children in all the schools. In this year additional schools were opened at Sunbury and Geelong, 411 children being transferred from Prince's Bridge to the former and 160, all under the age of 6 years, were sent to Geelong. At Prince's Bridge at this time about 22% were sick, at Sunbury 15% and Geelong 10%, with a high prevalence of ophthalmia, particularly at Prince's Bridge (children were not sent from there to the other institutions unless declared healthy by the medical officer). Because of overcrowding at Prince's Bridge it was deemed advisable to remove some of the more severe cases to Sunbury, where they improved. By November 1866 the infection had declined and the cases were of a milder character. Unfortunately, a measles epidemic broke out in this month, and at one stage nearly 400 children were confined to their beds.

Victoria's chief medical officer, W. McCrea, inspected all 225 boys and 430 girls in the Prince's Bridge establishment in September 1865. 'They presented the appearance of being clean and well fed. They all said they had plenty to eat, and they were generally in very good condition'. There was a large consumption of wine, milk, eggs and other nutritious food, as the children being admitted were 'generally in a very low condition'. The medical situation was troublesome:

A great number of them were affected with scabies and eczema, but nearly all of them in rapid progress of cure. About forty were suffering from hooping cough, most of whom were getting over the complaint favorably. There were twenty cases of ophthalmia, 12 which were severe, and the rest slight; many others had suffered from the disease and recovered. Twelve were suffering from diarrhoea; a few of these were bad cases, and accompanied by a good deal of debility. About twelve had chilblains; none of these very bad. Nine were suffering from debility after other diseases, and were progressing very favorably under a liberal administration of medical comfort. Three were suffering from gastric fever, and three from a scorbutic disease of the mouth.

Almost all the children had scabies on admission. The chief defect was want of accommodation to allow the separation and classification needed to eradicate skin diseases.

Ophthalmia flared up later in the year, and one ward was set aside for patients with this condition. A medical officer gave a good clinical description of cases of all grades of severity and went on: 'I have no doubt but that direct contact of the matter from diseased to sound eyes has produced it more than once. Some of the nurses have most certainly been inoculated in this way. The children bathing their eyes in the same water (this it was almost impossible to hinder at first) had, I think, a tendency to increase the severity of the affection.' He found the only effective treatment to be separation, darkened wards, a silver-lard ointment applied with a camel-hair pencil, unremitting attention to cleanliness, and removal of the pus with a sponge and warm water. Of 31 cases arising in the 160 children transferred to Geelong, 17 were mild, 6 showed some loss of vision which might be expected to recover and 8 were expected to have permanent loss of sight in one or both eyes.

A board of inquiry in 1865 found much to criticise in the accommodation at Prince's Bridge, particularly in regard to the privies, but it commended the physical appearance and attitudes of the children, who were clean and generally healthy, although some had a whoop. There were 11 cases of colonial fever, probably typhoid, and 3 of scarlet fever, the total number of sick amounting to 61, or about 10% of the children in the establishment. The clothing and bedding were adequate and clean, but owing to overcrowding there were often two children in one bed; the food and its preparation were satisfactory. The Board recommended that a progressive record be kept of both the physical and educational development of the children.

The reasons for the relatively high mortality in industrial schools become apparent when the age distribution of those admitted is considered. The data for the years 1873 and 1874, when a total of over 1,400 children was admitted, indicate that 6% were less than 1 year, with approximately 5% in each year of age up to the age of 9 and 7-11% in each year of age up to 15. The contemporary reasons given for the high mortality were the absolute obligation of the institution to take all candidates for admission (even if in the midst of an epidemic of infectious disease or if the child were sick), and the fact that many of the children, particularly the infants, were in poor health at the time of admission. About two-thirds of the children under 1 year were 'placed out to wet nurse', presumably implying that most infants below the age of weaning were so treated, a practice which was probably condoned only on the grounds of expediency. The mothers of some of the children were employed as nurses and generally found to be efficient and conscientious. Wet nurses were paid, but as this could lead to the neglect of their own child, employment was later limited to mothers who had lost a child. The age group most at risk may be deduced from the fact that 17% of admissions were aged less than 5 years, whereas this age group comprised only about 2% of those currently in the institution at any point in time.

The reasons for admission throw some light on the social problems of the period. Both parents were dead or in gaol in 8% of admissions, and nearly 10% of the children had parents who had deserted or could not otherwise support them. The mother with a dead or deserted husband, unable to support her child, accounted for 17% of admissions. The mother was dead and the father in gaol, had deserted or was unable to support the child in 11%. The father was in employment, and could presumably contribute to the support of the child, in about 8%. The father of the child was unknown in 4%, perhaps not surprising when 3% of the mothers were recognised prostitutes. A more surprising finding is that 4% of the admitted children had a lunatic as a father or mother. There are isolated entries which clearly spell tragedy, such as the child whose father had lost both arms and whose mother was dead.

The young children at Geelong underwent infant school training, and others up to the age of 9 years were required to attend school for the whole day. Those over that age spent half of their time at school and the remainder of their time was in some way usefully employed, after due allowance for play. The chief practical employments taught were tailoring, carpentry, dairy work, baking and cooking, blacksmithing and farm and garden work. The girls were taught to cook, wash, sew, keep their apartments clean and undergo training as servants. There were weekly visits by clergymen of all denominations and the teachers conducted Sunday schools as well as daily religious instruction. On week days there were other visits by ladies and gentlemen who 'addressed the children, exhibited magic lanterns for their amusement ... occasionally providing for them feasts, and supplying toys and books'. Footballs, cricket bats, gymnasia and other 'diversions' were provided.

The industrial schools appear to have been major paediatric institutions within their period of popularity in the third quarter of the nineteenth century. Like the Randwick Asylum, they were probably as well conducted as possible in the circumstances. The medical supervision seems to have been good, and it is notable that in Victoria expenses for medical comforts amounted to £1 or more per year per child, no insignificant sum in relation to the total expenditure. Whereas, with institutions such as the Ashfield Infants' Home, the children's hospitals as they were founded, and the Randwick Asylum, it was possible to keep the mortality down by declining admission, for understandable reasons, to those who might introduce infectious or contagious disease, this was not possible for the industrial schools, which also had to admit the foundlings in the absence of an institution such as the Ashfield Home. Their episodically high mortality and relatively high morbidity must be viewed in the light of these difficulties, and also the periodic overcrowding which was only relieved by the adoption of the boarding-out system. Within these limitations, the medical care was conscientious and the overall supervision sound, although doubtless with occasional exceptions. The system of divided control of many government subsidised or supported charities led to conflict, as previously indicated, and this certainly arose in relation to the industrial schools in Victoria in 1880.

The institutions discussed in this chapter represent, even more than the female factories, pioneering endeavour in paediatric care in this country. Modern social historians tend to decry them, largely on the basis of opinion evidence in official reports, newspaper discussions and individual comments to the effect that the children were impersonally treated and 'institutionalised'. Official reports of investigations of complaints reveal that these were often unfounded; newspapers have not changed. However, as much emphasis must be given to their positive medical achievement as to their negative psychological impact, an argument which may be seen as the direct descendant of the contemporary attitude that they enabled children to survive who would otherwise have died. It is more than this, for there is remarkable unanimity that the apprenticeship system after the age of 12 years was successful, an observation applying as much to Victoria's industrial schools, with their content of delinquents, as to Sydney's Randwick Asylum. Granting an adverse psychological effect of institutions (and there is not contemporary unanimity on this), it was apparently not permanent, and the children survived an experience which may have been traumatic and less than ideal without loss of ability to adapt to the wider world. It remains true that the boarding-out system was probably superior, as the potential evils appear to have been avoided by adequate supervision, although it is doubtful whether this system contributed much to infant survival.

Was the medical achievement acceptable? A precise answer to this query, leaving aside its psychological aspects, requires a comparison of mortality, or survival, rates between institutionalised children and those born into the general population, perhaps with due allowance for the fact that the former group necessarily came from an underprivileged class. Published data do not allow more than an informed guess, but archival material may exist to permit more precise evaluation. Infant mortality was generally high, and probably unavoidably higher in institutions obliged to admit infants, irrespective of the manner of feeding. Infant mortality was lower in institutions specialising in infant care where it was feasible predominantly to use breast feeding. The risks of putting infants in institutions were so well-recognised that the practice of not admitting them was followed, not only by the Randwick and Benevolent Asylums, but also by the newly developing paediatric hospitals in their earlier years. Mortality in later childhood, especially in relation to health status on admission, seems to have been very satisfactory. The records indicate that the medical care was of a high standard in the context of the times, and that the medical officers took pride in the health status of the children and in an acceptable mortality record. Certainly medical attention was more readily available in the institutions than to the children of the poor outside. Any excess morbidity in the institutions is attributable to overcrowding and inadequate hygiene. Epidemics were inevitable, especially in institutions compelled to admit suspected cases of infectious and contagious disease. When isolation methods could be applied, community epidemics were frequently kept out of the child institutions; this was a problem which the conventional children's hospitals also had to grapple with in a restrictive way, especially in outpatients departments. In one sense, these problems led to a demand for yet another kind of institution, the infectious diseases hospital, as advocated by D.A. Gresswell in Melbourne in 1890. The Queen's Memorial Infectious Diseases Hospital was established as a result in 1904 at Fairfield, and by 1914 was financed jointly by the state government and the municipalities. The Coast Hospital, established some years earlier, served a similar purpose in Sydney.

References and further reading

Brown, J. *op. cit.* Chapter 3.
Coulter, J. *Randwick Asylum: an historical review of the Society for the Relief of Destitute Children from the year 1852 up to ... 1915.* Sydney, 1917.
Ford, F.T. West. A report upon the Protestant Orphan Asylum, Emerald Hill. *Australian Medical Journal,* 1860, 5: 102.
Ford, F.T. West. Statistics of the Protestant Orphan Asylum, Emerald Hill... December 1859, to September 1862. *Australian Medical Journal,* 1862, 7: 313.
Hall, E.S. On the medical topography and vital statistics of the city of Hobarton, Tasmania, and its southern sub-districts, for 1855. *Australian Medical Journal,* 1857, 2: 81.

14 A CHANGING SOCIETY AND THE INFANT WELFARE MOVEMENT

Pray be careful that you don't disturb the baby's soft repose,
And you'll find his feeding bottle close beside his little nose!

P. Luftig, *The Woman of the Future, c.* 1895

The favourable trend in infant mortality at the turn of the century has already been reviewed (Chapter 10). In all states at about this period legislative measures directly or indirectly concerned with child health were passed; these included health acts, pure food acts and acts concerned with the provision of sanitation and water supplies. Steps were taken to ensure a purer milk supply (bacteriology was coming into its own as an investigative and monitoring procedure in public health) and establish effective dairy supervision, together with the elimination of tuberculous cattle by tuberculin testing — at least one paediatric institution was obliged to get rid of the infected cows which had hitherto supplied the children's milk. More effective notification of infectious diseases by medical certification was required, and some uniformity evolved between states, although a wider range of diseases was covered in Queensland, South Australia, Western Australia and Tasmania than in Victoria and particularly New South Wales. These advances in public health, together with measures specifically concerned with the care and welfare of disadvantaged children, ensured that the period 1890-1920 was one of more comprehensive and effective government interest in child health than ever before. Nonetheless, the suggestion that the replacement of the horse by the motor car was the major factor in the decline of gastroenteritis cannot wholly be denied.

The changes betokened changing social attitudes and pressures, and an increasing public awareness of personal and community responsibilities in preserving health. The economic depression of the 1890s, more than other recessions early in the century, led to an appreciation that the poor were not always poor through their own deficiencies of character and application. It was difficult to blame the indigence of children on improvidence, intemperance and other vices, the conventional 'causes' of poverty amongst adults. Similarly, the children could scarcely be expected to demonstrate in any effective way the contrary virtues of 'diligence, prudence, sobriety, thrift and initiative' with which a forward-looking working class should be imbued — although a little initiative, not necessarily socially productive, must have been required for some of the waifs and strays to survive.

It may or may not be that the convicts and underprivileged Irish in the New South Wales and Tasmanian communities lent a semblance of support in 1850 to these concepts of poverty, but by 1900 the widespread aversion to any social measures resembling the English poor laws was being replaced by more sophisticated approaches to social legislation. Charity offered to the able-bodied was not so uniformly regarded as a threat to independence, and again this view could scarcely be applied to children. Social progress may be seen as making its way tentatively, but at least initially, through attention to the problems of children who could do little to help themselves.

Thus, by the end of the nineteenth century it was generally accepted that the government had a responsibility not only to clothe, feed and educate children but also a moral obligation to provide them with an appropriate background for becoming respectable, useful and independent members of society; expenditure on these grounds was partly justified by the saving if children were prevented from becoming ne'er-do-wells or criminals.

It has been said, not without some justification, that the interest in the health of women, and in particular in their working conditions, during the latter half of the century was conditioned by concern over their ability to bear healthy children and so ensure a productive labour force. This economic motivation for social reform cannot be seen, at least to the same degree, in the rapid development of interest in the health and welfare of children. The general social concern is manifest in the works of Charles Dickens and Charles Kingsley; Henry Lawson's Little 'Arvie is the Australian counterpart of some of their juvenile characters. The increasing concern of the medical profession was almost entirely humanitarian, whereas in relation to the welfare of women it indicated as much concern for the future of society as for the women themselves. There was of course an increasing and appropriate concern with the unsatisfactory physique, hygiene and health standards of school children, as revealed by occasional surveys at about the turn of the century. Except for smallpox vaccination, the medical inspection of school children was the first major inroad made by the state into what had been regarded as private medical practice and the domain of the general practitioner, but occasional protests were muted.

Public interest in the whole subject of infant welfare is exemplified by an authoritative article in a popular journal, *The Lone Hand* (1909). The anonymous author pointed out that it was simplistic to compare Australia's relatively satisfactory infant mortality with Europe, where there was more poverty, more female factory labour, and more primitive living conditions in mediaeval cities, whereas the Australian people were probably the richest in the world, with every opportunity for health. It was suggested, rightly or wrongly, that preventable infantile illness left a high proportion of the children frail or in some way disabled, and that the greater proportion of the death rate was thus contributed from working class households in the cities. As indicated by overseas studies, most deaths occurred in artificially fed infants, and the mortality of breast-fed infants rose only slightly during the summer months by comparison with artificially fed infants. Hence the article argued that the first secret in the prevention and limitation of infant deaths was breast feeding; weaning in the summer months should be avoided. According to this article, probably 50% of Australian mothers did not breast feed. The second secret of prevention was the provision of 'clean' food for the child who could not be breast fed. That many infant deaths from infectious diseases were due to the older school child emphasised the need for proper hygiene measures. All these considerations required better education of mothers. Attempts to educate working-class mothers by means of lectures and pamphlets, visitations by philanthropic ladies and newspaper articles had failed, and municipal milk depots for supplying sterilized milk had done only a little good — they were often no more than a handy source of a bottle for bringing home the beer or for use as a weapon in domestic disputes. To be properly effective, inspection of the infants as a condition of getting the milk was required. The necessary maternal education was best provided by home visits by trained personnel, either voluntary or paid. The article observed that the problem of infant life protection was being tackled in a preliminary way in Australia but there was 'too much of the milk depot, the crèche, and the female inspector; too little of the development of the maternal spirit and of an instructed intelligence to guide it'. Both in moral terms and practical value these methods were inferior to that of home visits by experts.

The development of infant welfare organisations, usually initiated by voluntary action but ultimately government sponsored or controlled, in the first two decades of the present century was an inevitable step. The advisory clinics established by these groups did meet with some opposition on the grounds that they constituted an intrusion into private medical practice, which indeed they were. However, as with other state medical services, such as compulsory immunisation, they filled a need not adequately covered by conventional medical practice, and they were led, or supported, by prominent physicians, such as Wood, Turner and Vera Scantlebury Brown, concerned with paediatrics, whose integrity and dedication were unquestioned. The risk that trained nurses might replace the doctor in a significant segment of child care did not eventuate, although in more recent years some problems arose with the suggestion that infant welfare teaching in the centres had become too rigid, ritualistic and authoritarian. For the most part, the principle that the clinic nursing staff should refer sick children to medical practitioners was followed, but the problem was resolved somewhat differently in the several states.

Infant welfare was first systematically tackled in Australia by W.G. Armstrong. Prior to his appointment in 1898 as medical officer of health for Sydney, Armstrong had studied problems of infant mortality and welfare in England and France. In 1904, impressed more by the need to educate mothers, especially young mothers, in mothercraft, and by the need for emphasis on breast feeding rather than improving the milk supply, he employed a trained health visitor to visit and instruct mothers of all newborn babies in the city. Over the decade in which Armstrong pursued this policy, the proportion of breast-fed children rose from 72% in 1904 to 94% in 1914, whilst the mortality fell from 116 per 1,000 births to 68 per 1,000 births. One effect of the introduction of the baby bonus of £5 in 1912 was the reduction in the time between a birth and its registration from five weeks to three, a factor which may have had a favourable influence on his figures.

Armstrong paid tribute to the Alice Rawson School for Mothers, which was established in Sydney in 1908 under the auspices of the National Council of Women and immediately gained some government subsidy. It acted as a baby health centre and also provided some visiting by trained nurses. In 1913 the Lady Edeline Hospital was established at Greycliffe, Vaucluse, specifically for the treatment of babies with gastroenteritis, and a follow-up clinic was also provided; in 1934, as this disease declined, it was converted to a mothercraft home. The system was extended under government auspices in 1914, and baby clinics were established in a number of selected districts, each with an honorary physician and two nurses. Diseases were not to be treated, and sick babies were to be referred to hospital or to a doctor. The first clinic outside Sydney and Newcastle was established at Broken Hill in 1918, by which time there were 28 clinics throughout the state. In this year the Royal Society for the Welfare of Mothers and Babies was established with government assistance, and this produced an active publicity campaign. The Baby Clinics Board, under the chairmanship of C.P.B. Clubbe, became a committee of this Society; it included Dr. W.F. Litchfield and Dr. Margaret Harper. Dr. Harper examined the Truby King system instituted in New Zealand in 1907, and on her return the Tresillian Mothercraft Training Home was established at Petersham with her as medical director. Nurses came from other states for training in this institution, and all baby clinic nurses were required to train there. Other objectives were the care of babies with nutritional problems and, interestingly, behavioural disorders. Two further training homes were established in 1927 and 1937. By this time Truby King was protesting that his principles were not being followed by Margaret Harper, who maintained that the New Zealand environment was different. Scientifically, and in retrospect, the differences were minor, but smaller organisations grew up in New South Wales and Victoria which followed the King system more closely. In 1926 the baby clinics became a direct responsibility of the Director-General of Public Health. By 1939 there were over 200 infant welfare centres throughout New South Wales, and the infant mortality rate had gradually fallen to 39 per 1,000 births. In 1905, the Day Nursery Association opened the first crèche for working mothers. The Benevolent Society in 1911 established the Renwick Hospital for infants, and this was associated with an infants' outpatient department already existing at the Royal Hospital for Women. This hospital outlived its usefulness for infants, and in 1964, as a reflection of modern problems, it was adapted for the care of mentally handicapped children.

Another early development occurred in Adelaide, where the medical officer of health, Thomas Borthwick, introduced a programme similar to Armstrong's in 1907, but this was short-lived. Dr. Helen Mayo returned to Adelaide after studying paediatrics at Great Ormond Street in London, and in 1909 she was one of the prime movers in establishing a School for Mothers, later (1927) to become the Mothers and Babies Health Association.

The infant welfare service in Victoria began as a voluntary activity when Dr. Isobel Younger Ross established the first baby health centre in Richmond in 1917. Dr. Vera Scantlebury Brown became the first full-time* medical officer and the government's Director of Infant Welfare in 1926, by which time there were nearly 70 infant welfare centres. She began a training course for nurses, and later instituted prenatal clinics as a departmental function.

In Queensland four baby clinic centres were opened in 1918, and A.J. Turner became the first (part-time) director of this service in 1926. A training school in child welfare was founded in 1924, and a mothercraft association in 1931. The Western Australian (1923) and Tasmanian movements were established in the same period.

In 1910, shortly after visiting J.W. Ballantyne's pioneer antenatal clinic at Edinburgh, Dr. G. Wilson established an antenatal clinic at the Adelaide Hospital, but this ceased to function during the war. The first antenatal clinic in New South Wales was developed in 1912 by J.C. Windeyer, professor of obstetrics, in collaboration with P.L. Hipsley, at the Royal Hospital for Women, Paddington. During the first two years nearly 30% of the mothers subsequently confined in the hospital attended on at least one occasion. The routine investigations were for urinary protein, malpresentations and contracted pelvis, but these were extended to include blood pressure estimations in 1926; routine serological tests for syphilis were not included until 1937. The contribution of antenatal care to infant mortality gained in relative importance as mortality from post-natal causes declined.

At a later date many other organisations contributed to child health and welfare. The Country Women's Association was first established in New South Wales in 1922, based on overseas models. The Association was concerned with the welfare of women and children in the country, with special attention to educational

* Nominally, as a married woman, she was not full-time.

facilities for country children. It helped provide baby health centres in country towns, offered education on health, hygiene and first aid in the home, and established hospitals for children attending schools in towns, as well as children's playgrounds. The Far West Children's Health Scheme (1924) also offered baby health services staffed by nurses. Similar functions were instituted in Queensland by the Bush Children's Health Scheme under the auspices of the Australian Inland Mission. Although preceded by a district nursing system in South Australia in 1893 and in Melbourne about the same time, the distinctively Australian Bush Nursing Association developed between 1909 and 1914, largely through the leadership of Dr. J.W. (later Sir James) Barrett, who was honorary secretary from 1911 until his death in 1945, and whose paediatric interests have already been noted.

A further step in the evolution of infant and child welfare services may be seen in the recent pre-school health service evolved in Western Australia through the collaboration of the University Department of Child Health, the government Infant Health Service and the Australian College of General Practitioners. Infant health visitors undertake parental visits after the birth of the child, the chief objects being education and encouragement to attend a family medical practitioner at regular intervals. Historically, the involvement of private practitioners may eventually be seen as a significant advance in modern general practice, and particularly its integration with the government-sponsored health services, which took over the administration of the scheme in 1961.

Not all welfare was concerned with infants, and organisations concerned with the welfare, and especially the recreation, of youth also evolved apace during the present century. The Try Boys Society was founded in Victoria in 1883, to mention an early isolated example of many small voluntary organisations. The Young Men's Christian Association was first established in Australia in Adelaide as early as 1850, rapidly spreading to other states. The Young Women's Christian Association, beginning in Britain in 1855, did not reach Australia until 1880. Youth camps are typified by those of the Far West Children's Scheme in Sydney and the Lord Mayor's Children's Holiday Camp at Portsea, but these have also been conducted by some schools and churches since before the second world war. The police boys' club movement originated in Sydney in 1937, and the Youth Hostels Association in 1939. Legacy commenced after the 1914-18 war to take a paternal interest in the children of deceased ex-servicement. The Young Australia League, a non-denominational organisation, spread eastwards from Western Australia after 1905; it included girls from 1933. The National Fitness Movement, inaugurated by the Commonwealth Department of Health in 1939, serves as a reminder of the post-war emphasis on sport (with a socially interesting but delightfully simplistic attempt to diminish the competitive element), and on a wide variety of outdoor and 'adventure' activities. Schools have accepted an increased responsibility not only for physical fitness but also for health education, although to judge by some schools broadcasts from the Australian Broadcasting Commission these are more doctrinaire than profound or stimulating. The failure of Australian anti-smoking campaigns directed at children illustrates both the scope and the challenge for further development in health education.

References and further reading

Armstrong, W.G. The infant welfare movement in Australia. *Medical Journal of Australia,* 1939, 2: 641.
Cohen, L. *Dr. Margaret Harper: her achievements and place in the history of Australia.* Sydney, 1971.
Cope, I. Fifty years of antenatal care. *The Lamp,* 1962, vol. 19, no.8: 12.

15 CHILD MORTALITY IN THE TWENTIETH CENTURY

'The childer', ah! they grew and grew — sound,
rosy-cheeked, and tall:
'The childer' still they are to her. Old Granny
'minds them all'.

J.S. Nielson, *Old Granny Sullivan, c.* 1918

At the risk of some repetition, a summary of infant and child mortality in the twentieth century serves to introduce discussion of the factors involved in the improved outlook for youth over the past century. Perhaps the conclusions of the New South Wales Royal Commission in 1904 on the decline of the birth rate and the causes of infant mortality provide an appropriate background. On the latter question, it referred to defective care by midwives, ill-health of mothers, want of maternal knowledge, inexpert infant feeding, poor infant food substitutes, inadequate domestic hygiene, misuse of drugs, infanticide and baby-farming.

Between 1900 and 1945 male infant mortality fell from 101 per 1,000 births to 39, and the female rate from 83 to 31. Age specific mortality rates in males 0-4 years declined from 46 per 1,000 in 1881-90 to 18 in 1931-40 and 11 in 1941-45; the respective figures for females are 40, 14 and 9. As is apparent from earlier discussion, much of this improvement, perhaps 80%, is due to a decline in mortality from the infectious diseases, and of this the decline in gastroenteritis and allied disorders accounts for about one-third. Infant mortality from the latter had more than halved by 1930 and continued to fall; the introduction of antibiotics had no demonstrable effect. The declining mortality from diphtheria continued steadily; the introduction of immunisation in 1926 and its relatively general adoption in the 1930s did not affect the mortality curve appreciably, but the relatively steep decline after 1944 to negligible levels may reflect the eventual reduction of the number of susceptible subjects to a critical level. Scarlet fever mortality, already low, fell further prior to the introduction of antibiotics. Mortality from measles halved; as with diphtheria and scarlet fever, mortality was highest in the second year of life. Infant mortality from whooping cough declined steadily, also apparently independent of antibiotic therapy. The introduction of effective vaccine has eliminated the disease; a sequel has been the reduction in new cases of bronchiectasis. Antibiotics do appear to have accelerated the decreasing childhood mortality from respiratory diseases, which halved in all childhood age groups.

Mortality from tuberculosis in infancy and childhood was declining for many years before the introduction of effective chemotherapy, which was associated with a general decrease in mortality from this disease. Congenital syphilis ceased to be a significant cause of death after the third decade of the century. Other diseases to show a significant decline, although not numerically of major importance, are tetanus neonatorum (c.1920), appendicitis and hernia, erisypelas and pyogenic infections, all of a surgical character. Accidents in the first half of the century produced about 5% of all deaths in the 0-4 years age group, but amongst older boys this proportion was 25%, by comparison with 14% in girls. There was some decline over this period in the younger age group but little change in those aged 5-14 years. By comparison with the late nineteenth century, mortality from burns, scalds and drownings showed some reduction, although all three, together with accidental poisoning, remain significant. Motor vehicle accidents are an important additional factor in traumatic infant mortality, and also of course in the vulnerable 15-24 years age group.

Mortality from poliomyelitis became identifiable in 1921-1930, although major epidemics, doubtless causing some deaths, were recorded from 1908. The deaths per million were 23, 11 and 5 in the age groups 0-4 years, 5-14 years and 15-24 years, with a shift towards increasing mortality in the older age groups over the next two decades. Cerebrospinal meningitis, which occurred in epidemic form in both world wars, caused 2 deaths per 1,000 in the first two years of life prior to 1920, but mortality declined at all ages before the introduction of chemotherapy. Mortality from congenital malformations, cancer and leukaemia has probably shown no material change although relatively increased because of lessened mortality from other causes. Finally, as perhaps of social significance, there has been a recent increase in juvenile suicide.

Woodruff, dealing with South Australian experience, highlights the changed pattern of mortality by pointing out that formerly half the deaths in Adelaide were in children less than 2 years old, although this age group comprised less than 10% of the population. Nearly half of these deaths were due to teething or gastrointestinal troubles. By 1901, in the 0-4 years age group gastrointestinal disorders were the chief cause of mortality, followed by respiratory infections and external violence; in the 5-9 years age group respiratory infections took pride of place, reflecting in part at least the decline in the other common infective causes of child deaths. By 1960, the major contribution to mortality in both age groups was made by external violence, perhaps, it may be reasonable to add, not entirely explicable on the grounds of the lessened importance of other causes.

Modern age specific mortality rates are approximately 20 per 1,000 under 1 year, 1 per 1,000 aged 1-4 years, 0.3-0.5 aged 5-14 years and 0.7-1.6 in those aged 15-19 years (the higher figure is for males). The challenge of neonatal mortality now emerged; as early as 1914 Springthorpe was pointing out that if an Australian infant lived longer than a week its prospects of continuing life were better than in Europe. Interest in antenatal care became evident at this period but an important contribution to these early deaths was made by illegitimate children. Their infant mortality rate fell from about 20% of ex-nuptial births in 1905 to 10% after the first world war and it had almost halved again by 1940, although still about double the nuptial rate. The factors involved are probably more social than medical. Thus, if the Royal Commission on the decline of the birth rate in New South Wales in 1904 was correct in attributing the high illegitimate mortality to separation of mother and child, then social attitudes influencing unmarried mothers to retain their babies become of primary importance. On the medical side, Margaret Harper, appointed as physician to a mothercraft department at the Royal Hospital for Women in 1928, was able to increase the survival rate of premature infants from 56% to 80% within two years. Incidentally, she and G.A. Kelsall (Perth) were pioneers of exchange transfusion in Australian infants. In New South Wales in the first decade of the twentieth century the size of the problem is shown by the fact that illegitimate births comprised about 7% of the total, although in other states, such as South Australia and Western Australia, this figure was only 4%. The illegitimate birth rate per 1,000 unmarried women did not fall significantly prior to 1910, and it fell mainly in the older age groups, leaving a teen-age problem which is still unresolved.

The fifty years from 1870 to 1920 virtually established the pattern of modern medical practice as the mortality peaks of the late nineteenth century steadily subsided. Irrespective of their mode of spread, nearly all the dangerous infections went into a decline; for some, such as whooping cough and diphtheria, it required only the reduction of the pool of susceptible subjects by mass immunisation to eliminate them. The period was one of remarkable development in medical science but before linking this with the improved mortality it must be stressed that there were also considerable social and economic changes. In fact, we are confronted with a series of intercorrelated phenomena, and it is not easy to point to one factor to which the improvement may be attributed.

Perhaps basic to the question was demographic change. Children comprised about 40% of the population about 1850, and by 1911 they formed only about 30%, with some corresponding changes in the rest of the age distribution. Burnet has emphasised the importance of the age distribution to overall mortality by drawing attention to the general tendency, on a logarithmic scale, for case fatality to decline linearly with age up to about 10-15 years, after which it usually rises. The birth rate fell very significantly, and the number of children born to a woman, as well as the number of children per family or household, also fell. For those diseases in which mortality was highest in the first two years of life (whooping cough, diphtheria and scarlet fever) the chances of a high death rate were much reduced by the absence from the household of an older child. A few diseases, notably poliomyelitis and hepatitis, perhaps also chicken pox and mumps, may have profited by this and other changes, in that asymptomatic infections in infancy no longer produced natural immunity.

Therapeutic developments appear to have played no major role in the reduction of any of the infectious diseases. Mortality fell as much in those diseases for which there was no effective treatment as in diphtheria, where antitoxin and tracheotomy were available for half the period. Chemotherapy dates only from the late 1930s in Australia, but except in the respiratory diseases it made little impression on mortality curves. This does not imply the ineffectiveness of these drugs; as with diphtheria antitoxin, the effect on individuals was important, but for the most part mortality had fallen to such low levels, or was already falling so markedly, that no deflection of a graphic trend is detectable. A similar situation pertains in relation to tuberculosis, or at least childhood tuberculosis.

Prophylaxis, in a medical rather than a hygienic sense, was available for diphtheria from the 1930s but appears to have made little impact initially; mortality from diseases such as measles and whooping cough, for which effective preventive or therapeutic measures were lacking, declined similarly. The ability to detect subjects susceptible to diphtheria and scarlet fever almost certainly reduced institutional epidemic morbidity and mortality in later years. BCG was not accepted early in this country, and mass vaccination against typhoid fever, although successful in the South African war, never seems to have been considered as a public health measure in the general population, presumably because it was probably never feasible. Prophylactic injections were a novel innovation for the population; it took time before they were accepted as a matter of course or before they could be accepted as a matter for legislation. The only precedent was smallpox vaccination, and yet this disease had not spread widely on the occasions when introduced — the dire warnings of the doctors in support of compulsory vaccination had failed to materialise in Sydney even when the disease got a foothold there in the 1880s.

The sanitary reform movement relied heavily on the miasmatic theory of disease, the development of 'toxic' effluvia from drains, cesspools and decomposing material, which were assumed to cause most of the common fevers. Attention has already been drawn to the significance of the controversy between the miasmatists and the contagionists, but for present purposes it is sufficient to point out that there was no close temporal correlation between the introduction of effective sewage systems and the decline in mortality, even from typhoid fever. This disease undoubtedly became prevalent in insanitary situations, such as temporary camps, newly developing towns or rapidly enlarging populations in industrial suburbs, but it required more than a reasonable water supply and effective sanitation to ensure its disappearance; an elegant and efficient toilet is no cure for unwashed hands and the unhygienic handling of food. Public health measures became fully effective as public education became effective, and not before; Harvey Sutton's dictum 'neither filth nor smell causes fever until the carrier adds the specific infection and water or flies act as vectors', incomplete as it was when written in 1931, was much too subtle for the nineteenth century.

Infantile gastroenteritis, under whatever name it masqueraded, constitutes a special problem. Breast feeding was encouraged by the medical profession throughout the whole period, but certainly with enhanced fervour after the 1880s. Coupled with this was an interest in the quality and purity of the supply of milk, and artificial foods; in many situations the water supply was becoming reasonable by the turn of the century. Problems of infantile scurvy and rickets with artificial feeding were recognised, and 'natural' feeding of children was advocated. These medical, or technical, considerations might have had less impact were it not, once again, for popular education, increased literacy, and considerable publicity in the lay press. Concern over the falling birth rate gave further incentive to the education of the public, and to emphasis on the need for teaching domestic hygiene in schools. The Australian Health Society, established in Melbourne in 1875, had anticipated this, with its posters for schools and a rhymed 'Sanitary Alphabet'; its objectives were to create an educated public opinion in sanitary matters, to assist the public to live in accordance with recognised hygienic rules, and the removal of noxious influences deleterious to public health. It is difficult today to appreciate the ignorance of the housewife of even Edwardian times in relation to nutrition; meals were a matter of filling the stomach and not of feeding the body. The apparent success of various institutes and individuals in treating childhood marasmus and debility seems explicable only on the basis of the sensible dietary advice which they usually gave. Dr. Alan Carroll's Child Study Association and its clinic, formed under distinguished patronage in 1903, was a remarkable example in its early years; his book on *Health and Longevity* would have helped a young housewife and mother until it became, after his death in 1911, a medium for proprietary preparations.

Even contemporary observers found it difficult to explain the decline in infant mortality due to gastroenteritis; no single factor appeared to be operative or identifiable. On this basis, Gordon has suggested that the virulence of the responsible organisms may have altered. This explanation is generally accepted as accounting for variations in scarlet fever mortality and its complications, and the differing strains of bacilli responsible for diphtheria account for some of the vagaries of its epidemiological behaviour. The opportunistic dependence of Salmonella organisms has been demonstrated in very recent epidemics associated with artificial foods, and it seems probable that infantile gastroenteritis declined largely because a variety of altered circumstances conspired to limit the opportunities for Salmonella and related organisms. These circumstances were probably predominantly social, with professional medical support acting as a catalyst.

In this discussion I have indicated only the more direct influences on child mortality, but this approach oversimplifies the problem. Economic considerations led to an increasing age at marriage for the female, with a consequent reduction in child-bearing potential; economic considerations perhaps also led to limitation in family size. Economic hardship (and there was depression in the 1890s, and unemployment in the cities) made malnutrition more likely, whilst a smaller family, rising wages and increasing leisure bettered the family environment. Illegitimacy, at least in the more mature age groups, tended to decline; the high infant mortality associated with it, together with the arts of infanticide and baby farming, were reduced, partly at least for legislative reasons. Legislation *per se* implies an altered sense of social responsibility, perhaps to be regarded as culminating in the maternity allowances of the second decade of the century, with the stimulus to the early notification of births as an important consequence. Whether there were better ways of spending money than in maternity allowances and child endowment, from a public health as distinct from a social welfare viewpoint, will never be known.

The contemporary information exists for a more profound analysis of the decline in mortality over the half-century under review; a dissection of the intercorrelated phenomena is not beyond the bounds of scholarly application. My aim has been merely to indicate that there is no simple or single answer to the problem such as is sometimes to be found in both social and medical histories.

References and further reading

Burnet, M. The pattern of disease in childhood. *Australasian Annals of Medicine,* 1952, 1: 93.
Lancaster, H.O. *See* references to Chapter 10.
Woodruff, P.S. Today's epidemics. *Good Health for South Australia,* 1970, no.135: 5.

16 SOME MODERN TRENDS

Our literature review brought us to the brink of modern developments in paediatrics with which it is not proposed to deal in detail in this work. To illustrate experience of comparatively recent years I have chosen several different types of problem, selected not so much for their particular Australian significance as to show the nature of changing trends in practice and some of the factors involved.

The outstanding infectious disease of the modern era was poliomyelitis. The work of Colin MacKenzie in this area was revolutionary in its time. As early as 1908 he advocated the avoidance of stretching paralysed muscles and early gentle movement after the acute stage was over. At about this time he introduced the concept of 're-education' of muscles, as well as the concept of rest in a position most appropriate for subsequent re-education. For this purpose he developed a system of splints, notably the abduction splints for management of deltoid paresis. Hembrow observed that it was a triumph for MacKenzie's principles when two-thirds of the paralysed patients in the epidemic of 1937-39 recovered without significant disability; 18% suffered only moderate disability which did not prevent them from earning a living, while the remainder were severely crippled. Poliomyelitis was also a disease which stimulated the unorthodox, and amongst these Sister Elizabeth Kenny achieved international standing. Her aetiology, pathogenesis and pathological physiology were inappropriate, but empirically it appears that her therapeutic methods in certain circumstances achieved a measure of success, and in some respects were not far from a concept of rest with re-education. She did stress active treatment with exercise, and in this sense her methods argued against prolonged immobilisation and the consequent risks of fibrosis and contracture.

Earlier, in 1931, MacFarlane Burnet, working with Jean (later Dame Jean) McNamara established, by transferring the disease to monkeys, that there were at least two strains of poliomyelitis, a finding of importance when, with further developments overseas, a vaccine was being planned. Vaccination against poliomyelitis became a reality in Australia in 1954, with a far shorter time interval between discovery and mass introduction than had obtained half a century earlier with diphtheria immunisation. There were nearly 2,000 cases of poliomyelitis in Australia in 1954, but within a decade the disease had been relegated to the past. During earlier epidemics, Bertram McCloskey had demonstrated a relationship between the clinical onset of poliomyelitis, the distribution of paralysis and prophylactic injections against pertussis and perhaps diphtheria, so that these, as well as tonsillectomy, were precluded during epidemic periods. The long-term management of patients during the recovery phase and the need for rehabilitation stimulated services in these areas, and in Victoria Jean McNamara was responsible not only for organising physiotherapy services but also for arranging them on an outpatient basis. An interesting feature in the most troublesome years of poliomyelitis was the development in at least one state of a consultative panel, a member of which was always available, without cost to the patient, with the object of ensuring early diagnosis. The disease also stimulated the development of skills and techniques in the management of respiratory paralysis, and occasionally, as at the Prince Henry Hospital, Sydney, the resources were later to form the basis of intensive care units.

Orthopaedic conditions attracted considerable interest towards the end of the nineteenth century. Diseases of the hip joint, tuberculosis of bones and joints, and osteomyelitis, as well as some orthopaedic deformities, all called for long-term management. This posed special problems, both inpatient and outpatient, for paediatric hospitals. As an example, an orthopaedic branch of the Children's Hospital in Melbourne, the Frankston Orthopaedic Hospital, was established in 1930, and in the same year at the Royal Alexandra Hospital for Children, Sydney, a school for physically handicapped children was formed in collaboration with the Department of Education. At that time, nine out of ten of the children were suffering from poliomyelitis, staphylococcal osteomyelitis, or bone tuberculosis. Tuberculosis was already showing its spontaneous decline and the advent of specific chemotherapy after the second world war further altered the picture by producing earlier cure and reducing the need for corrective surgery. Antibiotics in the post-war era changed the prognosis and management of osteomyelitis, although this disease was also becoming less common. The reasons for this are obscure, but possibly there was some change in the pattern of trauma in childhood (perhaps more children were wearing shoes), or better first aid treatment was given at home. For some years poliomyelitis was to make up for the loss of these patients, but by the 1960s less than half of the beds were required for the disorders originally treated. Sometimes beds formerly used in this way were employed for the long-term observation of patients with recurrent rheumatic fever and rheumatic carditis, bronchiectasis and persistent asthma. The Margaret Reid Home, established by the New South Wales Society for Crippled Children in 1937, followed this pattern.

It is puzzling that some chronic disorders of childhood, such as asthma and bronchiectasis, attracted so little attention in the earlier literature. A clinical diagnosis of bronchiectasis in childhood was in effect a condemnation to long-term invalidity, intermittent severe disability or, quite frequently, early death. There was no effective medical treatment until intensive daily postural drainage was introduced prior to the second world war, but this made comparatively little impact until developments in anaesthesia allowed more comprehensive thoracic surgery which, in Australia, evolved rapidly as a result of wartime experience. Physical therapy was a demonstrably valuable aid to the extensive surgery which was frequently involved; lobectomy was common, sometimes bilateral, and often associated, as techniques developed, with additional segmental resections. Pneumonectomy for this condition led to increasing interest not only in the anatomy of the opposite lung but also in its function; its capacity to develop and even literally to grow if surgery were performed at a young age was appreciated. The combination of surgery and physical therapy greatly improved the lives of these children. The development of contrast media facilitated the selection of cases for operation and determined the extent of resections. Using this technique to full advantage, Howard Williams and his colleagues in Melbourne described several patterns of bronchiectasis in childhood. Developments in antibiotics and in the bacteriology of bronchiectasis permitted rational chemotherapy, either on a short-term or a long-term basis and the appropriate integration of antibiotic therapy, surgery and physiotherapy was reaching maximum effectiveness just at the time when the incidence of bronchiectasis began to decline, probably as a result of control over whooping cough and the use of more active measures, including bronchoscopy, to re-inflate collapsed lobes from any cause. At the time, tetracycline was the most appropriate antibiotic, and, as reported in Western Australia, some stained teeth were the price which a number of children paid for a reduction in sputum purulence. Lung abscess was another condition in which the same therapeutic developments required integration into a rational form of management. Today, there is a generation of physicians and surgeons who are unfamiliar with 'laudable pus' as an everyday problem, and there are perhaps occasions when the lessons of the past are forgotten, particularly when antibiotic therapy is unsuccessful.

Tooth decay represents a 'minor' problem largely resolved by different means. Harvey Sutton stated that in 1909 over 95% of children, both in town and country, had carious teeth, and 30% had dental abscesses. Over 25% of young adults were rejected for service in the 1914-18 war, 'the standard being two pairs of biting teeth in apposition'. By the time of his paper in the 1930s, the teaching of dental hygiene and the educational influence of school dental clinics had reduced the proportion of school children requiring treatment to 70% and to 30% amongst adolescents. Cleanliness and the use of the tooth-brush were becoming universal. Since that period, dental supervision has become fully accepted as a parental as well as a government responsibility, and the latter has extended into the field of fluoridation of water supplies.

Mental illness, and mental health, have received scant attention in the present review, largely because interest and practical progress are of recent origin. In the nineteenth century children were incarcerated in institutions with adults — usually they were taken in simply because of a lunatic parent, or even to provide occupational therapy for adult patients. In the 1890s there was a dawning recognition of mentally retarded children as a special problem; Dawson observes that the depression obliged families 'to throw their idiot children and older imbeciles on the state'. The Victorian Kew Cottages for imbecile and feeble-minded children were opened in 1887, and more were built over the next five years. Dr. J.V. McCreery, the superintendent, was a pioneer in the training and education of these children, some of whom became employable. In the mid-1890s, Dr. John Fishbourne opened a day centre for retarded children, also in Melbourne, and he was later instrumental in establishing the Talbot Centre for Epileptics. Moves of this kind ultimately required government support, not only financially but also in accepting responsibility for education and later for other specialised facilities and services. Centres for spastic children evolved in similar fashion; a special clinic and school established at the Children's Hospital in Melbourne in 1940 was supported by the Spastic Children's Society and the Victorian Departments of Health and Education. Associations interested in promoting the welfare of crippled children, which developed between the wars, usually came to take an interest in 'mental cripples' as well, especially as physical disabilities and deformities declined in importance. Scientific interest in retarded children was aroused by R.J.A. Berry, professor of anatomy at the University of Melbourne, when in 1923 he began doing intelligence tests in an attempt to correlate the results with cranial capacity. This led to a clinic for backward and defective children at the Children's Hospital which was to fill an increasingly more important role in subsequent decades. In Sydney, the plight of mentally deficient children was publicised by C.K. Mackellar, still interested in child welfare at the close of a long career. The problem was slow to evoke interest or action; the first senior academic post in child psychiatry was not established until 1971 (at Sydney University). The impressive developments of recent years are outside the scope of this work, but their social and medical background well merit specialised historical study. It deserves mention that many of these developments are associated with progress in para-medical and ancillary services and with the acceptance of greater professional responsibilities by workers in these fields. This comprehensive and coordinated approach — usually, but perhaps unfortunately, termed a 'team' approach — is generally considered an important modern development in itself.

References and further reading

Brothers, C.R. *Early Victorian psychiatry, 1835-1905*. Melbourne, 1962.
Dawson, W.S. *Annals of psychiatry in New South Wales 1850-1900*. Sydney, n.d. (Typescript. Library of The Royal Australasian College of Physicians).
Hembrow, C. Sir Colin Mackenzie and his contribution to the treatment of poliomyelitis. *Medical Journal of Australia*, 1973, 1: 194.
Sutton, H. The Australian child and the progress of child welfare. *Medical Journal of Australia*, 1931, 2: 603.

17 THE MATURATION OF PAEDIATRICS IN AUSTRALIA

The origins of paediatrics as a recognised sphere of specialised interest have already been noted as apparent by the closing years of the nineteenth century, the years in which special hospitals for children were also developing. Nonetheless, there were disappointments; surprisingly, the average attendance at the paediatric section of the Australasian Medical Congress in 1890 was only six, and as a result the section fell into abeyance until 1908. In this year, the paediatric section of the Congress in Melbourne attracted over 60 participants, three times the expected number, and many visited the Children's Hospital after the Congress concluded.

Perhaps a factor in this paediatric renaissance was the informal establishment of the Melbourne Paediatric Society in 1906. The Society, based on the staff of the Children's Hospital, had social objectives which helped to create a fellowship valuable to the advancement of a young specialty, but its scientific endeavour over half a century was commendable. About ten meetings were held each year which were regularly well attended, and for many years its proceedings were duly edited and published in the *Medical Journal of Australia*. It was, directly or indirectly, largely through the impetus of members of this society that the Australian Paediatric Association was formed in 1950, when the Society at last saw fit to acquire a constitution. A paediatric section within the framework of the British (now Australian) Medical Association dates back to 1922 in New South Wales but the formation of an independent Association, with H.D. Stephens as its first president, was a landmark in the history of Australian paediatrics. Fortunately, it took place shortly before more participation was demanded of specialist groups in medical education and medico-social activities at a national level. A critical further step was taken in 1965 with the establishment of the *Australian Paediatric Journal.* Other than the reports of the Melbourne society's meetings, the only regular paediatric publication was the *Records* of the Adelaide Children's Hospital from 1947.

To earn a living solely in what was traditionally the general practitioner's field remained a problem well into the present century; as W.B. Macdonald has put it, caring for children cannot be as remunerative as caring for the affluent aged. Even between the wars, paediatricians of distinction, such as Howard Boyd Graham, found it economically advantageous to give anaesthetics early in their careers. V.L. Collins, discussing the evolution of payment of formerly honorary staff at the Royal Children's Hospital in Melbourne, and the development of full-time salaried specialist services, put the problem bluntly: by 1949 'it was clear that it was quite impossible to provide a first-class medical service under the honorary system'. The system evolved in Melbourne facilitated the expansion of paediatrics as a specialty as well as the training of paediatricians, and it ensured a general rise in the standards of paediatric care.

Formal teaching in paediatrics has a short history, but students first attended the Hospital for Sick Children, as it was then known, in Melbourne in 1876, where some tuition was offered, notably by William Snowball. The Hospital was recognised by the University in 1912, and the students were required to attend for two, later six, weeks and from 1922 for three months full-time. H.D. Stephens was the first lecturer appointed (1940) but Kate Campbell had been a clinical lecturer in infant welfare from the inception of the department of obstetrics in 1929. In Adelaide, Dr. E.W. Way was lecturer in obstetrics and diseases peculiar to women and children as far back as 1887. By 1896 the students were attending the Adelaide Children's Hospital although it was not until 1902 that they were required to attend a course of clinical instruction from A.A. Lendon in diseases of children. Matters evolved more slowly in Sydney; the Royal Alexandra Hospital for Children was not fully established as a teaching hospital until 1924, shortly after which a six weeks' attendance became obligatory. Prior to this, A.E. Mills, professor of medicine at the University of Sydney, took groups of students to the Infants Home at Ashfield, and there were occasional visits to the children's ward at the Royal Prince Alfred Hospital. Dr. R.B. Wade and Dr. Edgar Stephen were appointed as lecturers in the surgical and medical diseases of children. Margaret Harper, said to have been a shy teacher, became lecturer in mothercraft in the department of obstetrics and gynaecology in the University of Sydney in 1930; she and Kate Campbell were the first neonatal paediatricians to be appointed to obstetric hospitals in their respective cities. Helen Mayo acquired a similar appointment at the Queen Victoria Maternity Hospital in Adelaide, but not until 1940.

The first professor of child health in Australia was Lorimer Dods, appointed in 1950 when an Institute of Child Health was established with Commonwealth support in the School of Public Health and

Tropical Medicine at the University of Sydney. The position carried clinical and teaching responsibilities at the Royal Alexandra Hospital for Children. Dods later initiated moves to establish the Children's Medical Research Foundation in 1958. A clinical research unit had been created in 1946 by the Children's Hospital in Melbourne, and in 1960 this was incorporated as a research foundation linked with the University of Melbourne through its newly established Department of Paediatrics.

The second chair of child health offered in some respects an even more exciting challenge in that it was created in a new medical school in Perth in 1957. This enabled the incumbent, W.B. Macdonald, the scope to introduce an imaginative curriculum in paediatrics, closely modelled on the recommendations of an expert study group of the World Health Organization. Perhaps its most original feature was a new 're-integration' of paediatrics with the parent subjects of medicine, surgery and obstetrics, perhaps a reflection of the fact that the battle for recognition had been won. Within five or six years, all Australian universities with faculties of medicine had established chairs in child health or paediatrics, and in more recent medical schools chairs in this subject have been automatically created.

It is not proposed to attempt here the invidious task of reviewing modern research and publications but, in addition to their inherent value, their significant influence on clinical standards, undergraduate teaching and postgraduate training is surely beyond dispute. In this connection, the establishment of research foundations such as those in Melbourne, Sydney and Adelaide has been of inestimable importance, and all receive generous public support. Internationally recognised contributions to paediatric knowledge have been made, in Melbourne, in the fields of gastroenterology, genetics, respiratory diseases, haematology, fluid and electrolyte balance and the surgery of congenital malformations and tumours; in Sydney in neonatal physiology (especially of respiration), and the Wilson-Mikity syndrome, the epidemiology of rubella and its complications in infants, and in a variety of biochemical studies related to childhood disease, notably the mechanisms of drug induced haemolysis. Interests in Adelaide have centred on social and community problems in paediatrics, as for example, the battered baby syndrome and behavioural problems. A research unit specifically for the newborn was established by the Sydney foundation at the Women's Hospital in Crown Street in 1961; it may be said to have pioneered a more aggressive approach to the specific problems of individual premature babies based on physiological and biochemical measurements.

It is, of course, evident from earlier chapters that contributions to paediatrics of international, or at least national, significance, were made long before the creation of formal research units, and hopefully they will continue. Perhaps the earliest in the present century was Harry Swift's description of erythroedema (pink disease) in 1914, followed by Margaret Harper's differentiation of fibrocystic disease of the pancreas (mucoviscidosis) from coeliac disease (1930 and 1938). She was a remarkable clinical observer, credited also with the advocacy of surgery for hypertrophic pyloric stenosis as early as 1915, and with raising the possibility of congenital abnormalities following maternal rubella with Norman Gregg. In Melbourne, Kate Campbell possessed similar clinical acuity, as a result of which she related retrolental fibroplasia to intensive oxygen therapy (1952). Gregg's work on the occurrence of congenital cataracts and cardiac lesions following maternal rubella was published in 1942. Charles Swan headed an Adelaide group, which included Tostevin (who first noted the association with deaf mutism), which extended the range of associated abnormalities, and postulated a change in virulence of the virus as an explanation for the recent recognition of the problem. However, as mentioned previously, deaf mutism had been noted as an epidemic disorder many years earlier, and it is believed that there had been no major epidemic of rubella in Australia for perhaps two decades. David Pitt in Melbourne and Menser and her colleagues in Sydney later greatly extended these initial observations. The next major contribution to the causation of congenital disorders was W.G. McBride's recognition of maternal thalidomide intake as causing phocomelia (1961 and 1963). McBride later devoted a prize received from abroad for this work to a fund for research into the welfare of the foetus, a vast but inevitable change from the nineteenth-century emphasis on the need to study the causes of infant mortality.

Whilst these are the outstanding products of primarily clinical observation there are many others. One may mention almost at random the description of the first case of favism in Australia by J.D. Harley and L. Dods in 1957; such 'first cases' often have more significance than a case report would suggest, either by drawing attention to a problem which may not be rare in the community or by providing the stimulus to specific research (as in this instance). Inevitably there are numerous examples of these 'Australian firsts', be they diagnostic or therapeutic. There is also the 'first successful case', as, for example, F. Arden's description in 1946 of the rupture of the liver in a newborn infant treated by blood transfusion and laparotomy. There is the rare disease, as the report of M. Fowler and R.F. Carter of meningitis attributed to an amoeba previously thought to be non-pathogenic, or the extended concept of Cockayne's syndrome, an heredo-familial disorder of growth and development, elaborated by Macdonald and his colleagues in 1960. There is too the field of improvements in techniques and their application, such as T.E. Allen's use of prolonged endotracheal intubation in selected respiratory problems at the Children's Hospital in Adelaide, or Margaret McClelland's specialisation in anaesthetic techniques for children in Melbourne. Accepting that each of these represents a 'type' or *genre* of publication which necessarily has significance in the history of Australian paediatrics, I believe it more appropriate that a paediatrician should make a more comprehensive evaluation. The point to be made here is no more than that progress in paediatrics in Australia has been sufficient to stimulate further research and to contribute to higher standards of clinical practice and teaching, all operating towards postgraduate interest in the specialty and thus to its progressive development. The historical trends in paediatrics, with the decline in infectious diseases (leaving neonatal disorders, respiratory diseases and trauma as perhaps the main emergencies of paediatric practice) mean that the further evolution of the specialty may lie in the hands of practitioners cast in a somewhat different mould; their interests must lie more in social and familial disorders and in the management of chronic ill-health. As an indication of this one may point to the interests of university departments in these areas, and perhaps particularly to the problems of Aboriginal child health, which remains a problem of nineteenth-century magnitude, both socially and medically. Much of the modern research in all these areas is epidemiological in character, and perhaps special mention should be made of the pioneer work of this kind carried out by Clifford Jungfer in his child health survey of the Adelaide Hills area, commencing in 1939.

Finally, perhaps Australian paediatrics may be said to have come of age when it can boast of its own historians, notably H. Boyd Graham, P.L. Hipsley and A.J. Wood, from amongst those of an earlier generation. The reason that there is more useful historical coverage of some aspects of Australian paediatrics than of other specialties may be, I believe, the striking changes in medical practice among children within the lifetimes of the authors. Another reason may lie in the concept underlying the present work, namely that social changes are effectively reflected in the medically overt problems of childhood. It is no accident that the three major Australian works on public health, by Springthorpe (1914), Harvey Sutton (1944) and Douglas Gordon (1976) all devote much space to the welfare and diseases of children and infants. The present review, produced to mark the academic inauguration of a new venture, the Prince of Wales Children's Hospital, is intended as a contribution to a now firmly established Australian tradition in paediatrics, and, hopefully, as a stimulus to further studies of many socio-medical aspects of paediatric history with which it has dealt but lightly. Rubella is not the only feature of a remote country which might open up new avenues of thought in child welfare and childhood disorders.

References and further reading

Dods, L. 'As it was in the beginning': some notes on the prenatal and early postnatal history of the Australian Paediatric Association. *Australian Paediatric Journal,* 1968, 4: 204.

Appendix I

MAJOR HOSPITALS FOR CHILDREN

Paediatric hospitals in Australia, as elsewhere, faced similar problems, and in the main they evolved similar answers. Most of these difficulties have been illustrated or discussed in the body of this work, but a summary may serve to introduce the histories of individual institutions cited below.

To the early paediatric hospitals, chronic or incurable disease, sick infants, abandoned children, infectious diseases and the risk of intramural epidemics were major administrative problems. Wards or homes for patients with long-term disorders, improved infant feeding, and the admission of mothers with their babies, improved social welfare arrangements and the provision of isolation wards or blocks were amongst the required administrative measures. During the twentieth century, the chief administrative problems were related to the changing patterns of childhood disease, the rapid evolution of diagnostic and therapeutic resources, and the need to provide specialised services for both inpatients and outpatients. For most of the first century of their existence these institutions were largely financed and conducted by private charitable enterprise; government subsidisation was generally inconsistent. For the most part, their histories are a record of struggle, at times even for survival, but always to meet the needs of their communities.

Melbourne

The Melbourne Hospital for Sick Children, now the Royal Children's Hospital, was established in 1870, and occupied the former home of Sir Redmond Barry in Carlton from 1875 to 1963 when it moved to the present Parkville site.

> Carmichael, J. [Mrs. G. Mullis] *Hospital children: sketches of life and character in the Children's Hospital, Melbourne.* Melbourne, 1891.
>
> Gardner, L.B. *Royal Children's Hospital, Melbourne, 1870-1970.* Parkville, Victoria, 1970.
>
> Graham, H.B. Beacons on our way: some memories of the Children's Hospital, Melbourne. *Medical Journal of Australia,* 1953, 2: 517.
>
> Lake, J. ed. *Childhood in bud and blossom: a souvenir book of the Children's Hospital Bazaar.* Melbourne, 1900

Adelaide

The Adelaide Children's Hospital, first conceived in 1876, opened in 1879 in North Adelaide.

> Barbalet, M. *The Adelaide Children's Hospital 1876-1976.* Adelaide, 1976.

Brisbane

The Brisbane Hospital for Sick Children opened in 1878 and was transferred to its present site at Herston in 1883.

> Fison, D.C. *The history of the Royal Children's Hospital, Brisbane.* Brisbane, 1970.
>
> McConnel, M. *Our Children's Hospital.* Brisbane, 1897.

Sydney

The Sydney Hospital for Sick Children opened in Glebe in 1880. Now the Royal Alexandra Hospital for Children, it has been in operation at Camperdown since 1906.

> Hipsley, P.L. *Early history of the Royal Alexandra Hospital for Children, Sydney, 1880 to 1905.* Sydney, 1952.

> Steigrad, J. The achievements of the Royal Alexandra Hospital for Children. *Medical Journal of Australia,* 1965, 2: 813.

St. Margaret's Children's Hospital was opened in 1967 adjacent to St. Margaret's Hospital for Women, Darlinghurst.

The Prince of Wales Children's Hospital, the successor to a paediatric unit established at the Prince of Wales Hospital in 1964, first accepted patients in 1976 although not formally opened until 1977. Unlike the previous hospitals, which are associated with the University of Sydney, it is affiliated with the University of New South Wales.

Perth

After protracted discussions and planning extending over more than a decade, the Children's Hospital was officially opened in 1909. It became the Princess Margaret Hospital for Children in 1957.

> Clarkson, J.D. Princess Margaret Hospital for Children. *Royal Perth Hospital Journal,* 1964, 13: 613.

Hobart

A children's hospital was added to the General Hospital in Hobart in 1909.

> Seager, P.S. *Hobart General Hospital: an epitome of its history.* Hobart, 1921.

A number of major hospitals have had children's wards, the first, as far as we are aware, being the Melbourne Lying-in Hospital and Infirmary for Diseases of Women and Children (now the Royal Women's Hospital), which admitted children from 1861 to 1867.

Appendix II

UNIVERSITY DEPARTMENTS OF CHILD HEALTH OR PAEDIATRICS

1950 *University of Sydney (Child Health):* Sir Lorimer Dods, M.V.O., M.D., Ch.M., D.C.H. Lond., F.R.A.C.P., to 1960; T. Stapleton, M.A., D.M. Oxon., F.R.C.P., F.R.A.C.P.

1957 *University of Western Australia (Child Health):* W.B. Macdonald, M.D., F.R.A.C.P.

1959 *University of Melbourne (Paediatrics):* Vernon L. Collins, C.B.E., M.D., F.R.C.P., F.R.A.C.P., D.C.H. Lond., to 1974; D.M. Danks, M.D., F.R.A.C.P.

1959 *University of Adelaide (Child Health):* G.M. Maxwell, M.D., F.R.C.P., F.R.A.C.P.

1961 *University of Queensland (Child Health):* T.J. Rendle-Short, M.A., M.D., D.C.H. Lond., F.R.C.P., F.R.A.C.P.

1962 *University of New South Wales (Paediatrics):* John Beveridge, M.B., B.S., F.R.A.C.P.

1965 *Monash University (Paediatrics):* A.C.L. Clark, M.D., F.R.A.C.P.

1968 *University of Tasmania (Child Health):* Ian C. Lewis, M.D., F.R.C.P., D.C.H.

1975 *Flinders University of South Australia (Paediatrics):* G.M. Kneebone, M.B., B.S., M.Sc. Pittsburgh, F.R.A.C.P.

Select bibliography

The Australian Encyclopaedia. New ed. Sydney, 1958.

Bigge, J.T. *Report of the Commissioner of Inquiry into the State of the Colony of New South Wales.* London, 1822.

Bigge, J.T. *Report, etc., on Agriculture and Trade in New South Wales.* London, 1823.

Collins, D. *Account of the English colony in New South Wales, etc.* London, 1798.

Cope, I., Forster, F.M.C. & Simpson, S. *Obstetrics and gynaecology: short-title catalogue ... with references to these subjects in Australian and British journals published before 1900.* Sydney, 1973.

Cunningham, P. *Two years in New South Wales...* 2 vols. London, 1827.

Ford, E. *Bibliography of Australian medicine 1790-1900.* Sydney, 1976.

Forster, F.M.C. *Progress in obstetrics and gynaecology in Australia.* Sydney, 1967.

Franklin, Lady Jane. *Some private correspondence of Sir John and Lady Franklin (Tasmania, 1837-1845)* ed. by G. Mackaness. Australian Historical Monographs, vol. 15, Sydney, 1947.

Gandevia, B. *An annotated bibliography of the history of medicine in Australia.* Sydney, 1957.

Gordon, D. *Health, sickness and society: theoretical concepts in social and preventive medicine.* St. Lucia, Qld., 1976.

Historical Records of Australia. Sydney, 1914-1925.

Historical Records of New South Wales. Sydney, 1892-1901.

The Hobart Town Gazette and Southern Reporter: facsimile reproduction. Vols. 1-4, 1816-1819. Sydney, 1965-1967.

Hogan, T., Yarwood, A.T., & Ward, R. *Index to journal articles on Australian history.* Armidale, N.S.W., 1976.

Inglis, K.S. *The Australian colonists: an exploration of social history, 1788-1870.* Melbourne, 1974.

Lancaster, H.O. *Bibliography of vital statistics in Australia and New Zealand.* Glebe, N.S.W., 1964.

Lancaster, H.O. *Bibliography of vital statistics in Australia: a second list.* Glebe, N.S.W., 1973.

Lewis, M.J. *Populate or perish: aspects of infant and maternal health in Sydney, 1870-1939.* Ph.D. thesis, Australian National University, 1976.

Springthorpe, J.W. *Therapeutics, dietetics and hygiene.* Melbourne, 1914.

Sutton, H. *Lectures on preventive medicine.* Sydney, 1944.

The Sydney Gazette and New South Wales Advertiser: facsimile reproduction. Vols. 1-8, 1803-1810. Sydney, 1963-1970. Vol.9, 1811. Canberra, 1973.

INDEX

151